IMPERIAL TASTE

A Century of Elegance at Tokyo's Imperial Hotel

Nan and Ivan Lyons

KODANSHA INTERNATIONAL
Tokyo and New York

Recipes adapted for the home kitchen by the Imperial Hotel.

Cover: An Imperial feast set against the mural in the Old
 Imperial Bar.
Front endpapers: Imperial Hotel postcards featuring
 interiors of the first hotel, circa 1900.
Back endpapers: *Left,* the oldest surviving hotel plate,
 made around 1910. *Right*, Frank Lloyd Wright-
 designed plate.
Below: The Rendez-vous Lounge.

Cover and food photography by Yoshikatsu Saeki.
Photos of the present Imperial Hotel by Ryuzo Tanabe.
Book and cover design by Yozo Nakamori and Noriko
Sagesaka.
Food styling by Raisins, Inc.

Distributed in the United States by Kodansha Interna-
tional/USA Ltd., 114 Fifth Avenue, New York, New York
10011. Published by Kodansha International Ltd., 17-14,
Otowa 1-chome, Bunkyo-ku, Tokyo 112 and Kodansha
International/USA Ltd., 114 Fifth Avenue, New York,
New York 10011. Text copyright © 1990 by Nan and
Ivan Lyons. Recipes copyright © 1990 by the Imperial
Hotel. All rights reserved. Printed in Japan.

First edition, 1990

Library of Congress Cataloging-in-Publication Data

Lyons, Nan.
    Imperial taste: a century of elegance at Tokyo's
Imperial Hotel/Nan and Ivan Lyons.
        P.   cm.
    Includes index.
    1. Teikoku Hoteru—history. I. Lyons, Ivan. II. Title.
TX941. T4L98 1990   90-48570
647.9452'135—dc20   CIP

ISBN 4-7700-1513-5

CONTENTS

Introduction   7

The First Imperial   11

The Second Imperial   23

The Third Imperial   39

Imperial Service   47

Imperial Weddings   55

Imperial Kitchens   63

Imperial Restaurants   73

Imperial Recipes   89

Basic Recipes   166

Index   173

INTRODUCTION

t is no coincidence that the Imperial Hotel is in Tokyo. This is a hotel that could not exist anywhere else. It is as indigenous as the cherry tree.

Tokyo, however ancient its history, is a modern city. Hardly anything in it is more than a hundred years old. It is a new city built on old customs, the capital of nuance in a world that has all but forgotten subtlety. The Japanese are accomplished cultural acrobats: they juggle shades of attitude and tints of phrase as easily as chopsticks. Unlike in New York or Paris, what is visible in Tokyo does not reflect its heart. The heritage and pulse of the city are not to be found in skyscrapers or relics of the past. They are to be found in its people.

The principles of Japanese architecture were formulated on the premise of replacement rather than longevity. Plagued by earthquakes, fires, and floods, Japan developed what can be called an "architecture of resignation." Light wood and paper structures were relatively inexpensive and left neither rubble nor regret when lost in the wake of inevitable natural disasters. Shoji screens, tatami mats, pebbles in a garden—they were neither dangerous nor irreplace-

able. Not expecting structures to survive the people who built them, the Japanese developed an inner strength, an independence from the tangible. Realizing that the only thing they could control was themselves, they sought security in *social* structures.

However inevitable it was that Japan change in order to become part of the international scene, the changes made were not visceral. No matter how Westernized Japan has become, it is an accommodation rather than a catharsis. All change is on the surface, a form of personal architecture required of modern Japanese men and women. The inner landscape on which these new edifices are constructed is still Japanese soil.

As is the land on which the Imperial Hotel was built once, built twice, built thrice—each time more resolutely modern than before. What a glorious paradox: Conceived over a century ago as the country's first Western-style hotel, the hotel has succeeded because it is so totally Japanese.

The Imperial is the only hotel whose history is entwined with that of a great nation. Most often, hotels mirror what society wishes to see. The uniqueness of the Imperial is that it reflected what a society wished to become.

In order to appreciate the contemporary visual sweep of the Imperial Hotel, it is necessary to cross the broad boulevard known as Hibiya-dori and step back into Hibiya Park, which borders the Imperial Palace grounds. This is no mere travel tip: the hotel must be viewed in perspective.

No one enters the Imperial Hotel without a sense of anticipation. The lobby space is vast. Two stories high, it confirms even the loftiest of expectations. Supported by massive marble columns, and by its reputation as Tokyo's premier venue, the Imperial lobby produces and participates in hundreds of dramas daily. It is the Kabuki, the Colosseum, and the Old Vic all in one.

The cast includes Americans, Germans, Australians, Middle Eastern businessmen, and fainthearted ladies whose blood pres-

View from the mezzanine floor across the Rendez-vous Lounge to the Rendez-vous Bar; the lobby is on the right.

sure rises and falls according to the thickness of the lemon slices in their afternoon tea. Salesmen from Hamburg and Hokkaido read contracts across a table in the lobby lounge while a young couple read one another's eyes after making plans for their wedding at the hotel.

There is a sudden rush of activity as bellmen herd a flock of designer luggage. A movie star or a member of inherited royalty hurries by. Tourists from Norway, a trade delegation from France, and a group of smartly-dressed OL's (office ladies) all look up, less to catch a glimpse of the official entourage than to be seen themselves. However disparate their cultural and economic backgrounds, social boundaries cease to exist. Everyone has instant diplomatic immunity. They are citizens of the Imperial Hotel.

Amid the spaciousness of the lobby—all the more spectacular for being located in the heart of one of the most crowded cities on earth—semicircles of Japanese businessmen bow to each other like opposite ends of parentheses. An around-the-clock cavalcade of voguish women flaunts the complete inventory of feminine fashion from kimonos to culottes, while men hurry up and down the grand staircase wearing anything from morning coats to jogging suits. No matter what time of day or night, someone is always in formal dress. There is electricity in the air: the flash of disposable income and the crackle of investment capital amid whispers of consummate diplomacy. Eyes look up expectantly as a bellman pages a guest by holding a slate and sounding a gentle bell. Astonishingly, everyone in sight expects to see his name on the slate. As the bellman disappears, conversations resume in more languages than are spoken at the United Nations. To the observer, the lobby is an anachronism come to life—a very elegant cocktail party in a medieval village square.

The focus of the lobby—even more imposing than the grand staircase or the marble columns or the burnished metal map of the world displaying local times in key cities or the ever-changing floral displays—is an epic ceramic mural, "Dawn," by Minami Tada. It is a wall-to-wall, two-story-high creation that reflects not only the artist's vision but that of the hotel in commissioning so heroic a work. Incredibly, this "wall of light" does not dominate

The lobby paging system—a bellman carrying a sign and a bell.

View along the Rendez-vous Lounge's mural "Dawn," toward the Japanese-style garden at the entrance to the hotel.

the lobby so much as reflect it. The artist has written: "The wall of light symbolizes the break of dawn, showing the waves glittering in their seven colors in the morning sun and spreading from the seashore to the horizon behind—depicting the gradual and massive opening of the whole world."

An appropriate description, considering that some 20,000 people a day pass in and out of the Imperial. A far cry from a typical César Ritz hotel designed to discourage "people from the outside." First-time guests at the Ritz in Paris often seem confused as they enter the hotel, wondering if perhaps they have taken a wrong turn and missed the lobby altogether. In a fit of chic, Ritz decided that his hotel should recall a gentleman's town house. He knew that what made a hotel "grand" was more than hot showers and a reliable laundry. Responsive management makes a hotel "good." The fine art of anticipation makes a hotel "very good." But being "grand" has to do with more than hotel services—it has to do with *whom* the hotel services. The key ingredients, then as now, are the guests.

The few "grand" hotels that are left have survived the most volatile changes—political revolution, social upheaval, and shifting economies. They survive because, like Switzerland, they offer both neutrality and a high standard of living. But, unlike Switzerland, they offer also a blend of reality and illusion, past and present, high drama and serenity. The Ritz in Paris, the Savoy in London, the Waldorf-Astoria in New York, and the Imperial in Tokyo have become such integral parts of their local landscapes that they rival the sights of the cities in which they are located. It is possible to stay at any of them and never venture out the front door but still savor the essence of a world capital.

Geographically equidistant between the nobility of the Imperial Palace and the neon of the Ginza, the Imperial Hotel plays havoc with traditional borders of past and present. It is a place where old and new are separate, dependent, distant, connected. With the brilliant eye for detail that the Japanese have elevated to an art form, the Imperial has fine-tuned its style of hospitality into a specific taste.

One defines taste usually as an individual preference—or as the sense that distinguishes sweet from sour, bitter from salty— or as having a precise flavor. "Imperial taste" seduces the palate with a unique blend of yesterday and today.

The First Imperial

he earliest of overnight accommodations in Asia were "public houses"—empty huts placed at caravan stops. Most travel took the form of religious pilgrimages by missionaries and their followers. Dressed in white, carrying walking sticks, they made difficult and often dangerous journeys to visit holy sites: Buddhist and Shinto priests built temples and shrines in locations often as remote as they were beautiful.

In Japan, travel by people other than officials and pilgrims was rare until the Edo period (1603–1867), when a formal system of highways and facilities spawned the development of recreational travel. Stimulated by long periods of peace, exquisite geography, and a Japanese aesthetic that sought out natural beauty, all classes of people began making pilgrimages. Poets and historians published travel diaries describing their journeys, and places associated with specific poems were sought out by recreational travelers.

In the eighteenth century, more sightseers than religious disciples could be found along a network of highways that linked the provinces to the two main cities—Kyoto and Edo.

Everyday traffic on the highways was by foot. Only rice and farm produce were deemed important enough to ride in wheeled carts. Official messengers and members of the nobility were allowed on horseback, while the rich and royal were transported in sedan chairs. Therefore, travel was slow even as these well-maintained national walkways grew in importance. Mounds of earth marked the distance every few miles, and shade trees were planted along the road for comfort. The time it took to travel made for anything but a comfortable journey. Travelers were beset not only by physical and climatic

This print from Hiroshige's series *The 53 Stations of the Tokaido* shows fabric shops lining the road at Narumi, near Ise.

hazards, but by thieves and highwaymen who made the roads dangerous after dark. Still, for many Japanese, the highpoint of a trip was the journey itself: filled with danger and adventure, it offered people from small villages the opportunity to see a type of "street life" that was a microcosm of Japan. Roads were filled with royal processions, priests, entertainers, merchants selling exotic wares, and the opportunity for conversation with strangers from distant towns.

Spaced at convenient intervals along the road were resting places, stations, where travelers could spend the night—often with such amenities as a hot bath or an amorous companion. At first, these inns were run by farmers to supplement their income. They provided lodgings, readied fresh horses, and arranged for porters. As traffic increased, roads were widened and farsighted entrepreneurs invented the profession of innkeeping.

The artist Ando Hiroshige, in his series of woodblock prints titled *Fifty-three Stages of the Tokaido*, immortalized life on the highway going from Edo (now Tokyo) to Kyoto.

Edo had been a settlement since the twelfth century. It was the site of a strategic fortress built in 1457 by a warrior named Ota Dokan on high ground near the bay. But Edo, for all its military importance, did not come into prominence until 1603, when Tokugawa Ieyasu became shogun. Finding most of the city facing the bay, he proclaimed Edo ideal for his headquarters. He built a castle where the old fortress stood and began to fill in marshland that at high tide was underwater—the area that is today the world's most expensive piece of real estate: Ginza.

Edo developed into the nation's political center, although Kyoto would remain its capital until the Tokugawa family lost

power and the Meiji emperor regained control of Japan from the shogunate. In 1868, Edo would be renamed Tokyo—meaning "Eastern Capital."

It was the Tokugawa shogunate that gave Japan's fledgling hotel industry its greatest boost. The land had been divided among some 250 feudal lords (daimyo), each of whom was required to travel from his fiefdom to spend a portion of every other year in Edo attending the court of the shogun. The law even specified how many retainers were to be brought on each trip, their attire, and the route they were to take. To reduce possible conspiracy against the government and ensure peace close to the shogun, the daimyos' families were ordered to remain in Edo. The daimyo, with a vested interest in the comfort and

The early morning departure of a daimyo and his entourage from a *honjin* in Seki, a checkpoint between Ise and Lake Biwa. From *The 53 Stations of the Tokaido*.

Travellers on the Tokaido, with Mt. Fuji in the background. From *The 53 Stations of the Tokaido*.

safety of their loved ones, built elaborate mansions that added to the cachet of the new capital as a destination for sightseers.

The custom of making these annual journeys continued for over 200 years, providing Japanese life with one of its most spectacular sights—at any one time, moving at a stately pace along the national roads for all to see, there might be dozens of colorful, elaborately costumed corteges. The processions of the feudal lords required not only a vast number of inns but also a variety of accommodations. A powerful daimyo could not be expected to stay in the same type of room as his personal attendants, nor would someone of high rank or wealth accept lodgings that did not reflect his status in life. Thus, the Japanese grand hotel was born.

Three levels of inns were established at each station on all of the national highways. The most exclusive of these inns were called *honjin*, hotels built with the same style and craftsmanship as the daimyo mansions in Edo. Although large and imposing structures, their standards of service were so exacting that only ten guests could be accommodated at any one time. They were reserved exclusively for members of the imperial family, daimyo, high officials, and priests. Next came the *waki-honjin* (annex-*honjin*) for lower-level VIPs, or those for whom there was no room at the main inn. The lowest ranking members of a procession stayed with ordinary travelers at a lodging known as a *hatago*.

In order to accommodate the many travelers ranging from lords and ladies to gamblers and poets, a network of some 80,000 inns developed along the highways. On the great Tokaido alone, spanning the 300 miles from Kyoto to Edo, were 111 *honjin* hotels, 68 *waki-honjin*, and 2,905 *hatago*. As the peaceful decades

of the Tokugawa shogunate unfolded, traffic on the highways increased along with prosperity.

In the mid-1600s, fearing that European religious influences might encourage peasants to question the established order, Tokugawa Iemitsu, the third Tokugawa shogun, banished all foreigners from Japan. The only Western trade was with the Dutch: one ship a year was permitted to dock at Nagasaki. Japanese were not allowed to travel abroad. Those who lived in foreign countries were forbidden to return. Isolated from the West, and with a respect for traditions rather than trends, Japan, like the Japanese inn, preserved its heritage for many centuries—unchallenged by new ideas from outside its shores.

That would prove to be a problem.

Print made in 1890 showing the horse-drawn trams in Ginza. (Courtesy of Tokyo Gas)

In 1853, the US government sent Commodore Matthew Perry to Japan to open diplomatic and trade relations. Conflict between supporters of the shogunate, which had usurped the emperor's authority, and the daimyo who wished the imperial court returned to power, focused on whether to continue a policy of isolationism. The shogun wanted to open Japan to foreigners, with or without restoring the emperor to power. The daimyo who wanted the emperor's authority restored were divided on whether to establish economic ties to the West. The resulting conflict ended with the restoration of the monarchy in 1867. The new emperor titled his reign the "Meiji" era, a time of "enlightened rule." As though to put an end to its inward focus, the capital was moved closer to the ocean—from Kyoto to Tokyo. The Meiji emperor's goal was to transform Japan into a prosperous and strong country. Like Peter the Great, he was convinced that the only way to modernize his country was to look west.

But before Japan could become a world power, it would have to reenter the world. It was 1869 and the new Imperial government announced that Japan, after two centuries of isolation, was open for business and ready to welcome visitors.

Except for one thing. There was no place to stay.

In an age during which William Waldorf built his first hotel on Fifth Avenue, and impresario Richard D'Oyly Carte opened the Savoy in London as the ultimate in luxury, while world capitals competed with one another for new heights of lavishness, imperial Japan found itself without suitable accommodations for the international diplomats and industrialists with whom it hoped to do business.

The country's point of entry from abroad was Yokohama, which had the deep-sea port that Tokyo lacked. In 1872, the first railroad in Japan was built between Yokohama and the nation's new capital. Foreigners stepped off the train in Tokyo to find themselves in the Ginza, which literally means "Silver Mint," named after the area's most prestigious landmark. Since Ginza was where visitors would form their first impressions of Japan, the new regime was eager to make the area modern—and modern meant Western.

The Tokyo Tsukiji Hotel. Print by Hiroshige III made in about 1870. The Tsukiji Hotel stood from 1868 to 1870.

But there was no first-class Western-style hotel in Tokyo. All that existed was the Seiyoken Hotel in Tsukiji, the successor of Japan's first western-style hotel, the Tsukiji Hotel. Now the site of the largest fish market in Japan, Tsukiji was originally the area to which foreign visitors were restricted. Even as regulations relaxed and *gaijin* (foreigners) were permitted to travel outside of Tsukiji, there were no suitable accommodations for them. In 1887, a local English-language newspaper described the new Tokyo Hotel built in the Hibiya area as "an ugly comfortless barn, inferior, if inferiority be conceivable, to the Seiyoken." The best option for those who visited Tokyo was to return at night to Yokohama, where more satisfactory quarters could be found.

Foreign dignitaries who were guests of the Meiji government stayed at state-owned guest houses in Tokyo. The most famous of these was the Rokumeikan, a two-story brick building near the present site of the Imperial Hotel. The Rokumeikan, the official meeting place for the international set, operated as a club, a place to which the Japanese could take foreign guests and hold banquets in their honor. It was a venue that gave its name to an era: The Rokumeikan era during the early Meiji period came to symbolize rapid Westernization. Japanese couples dressed in new Western-style clothes danced to the same piano music that people were dancing to throughout Europe and America. However, the Rokumeikan was open only to official guests of the government and did not solve the problem of providing accommodations for lesser VIPs. During this period, other visitors stayed in luxurious but traditional inns known as *ryokan*.

The government understood the problem: As long as they offered tatami mats, visitors could not take them seriously. But Japan needed to be taken seriously in order to renegotiate treaties for trade routes.

The interior of a ryokan in Akasaka, Edo (now Tokyo) from *The 53 Stations of the Tokaido*.

Besides, the Japanese were a people with a heritage of innkeeping as well as a profound sense of hospitality and protocol. It was clear they had to provide rooms that would satisfy their guests' requirements—however strange those requirements might be. Many Japanese had been sent abroad to report on Western customs. Even though they were somewhat intimidated by the outside world, they knew that adopting Western customs was the fastest way for Japan to modernize.

Almost overnight, everything from manners and dress to food was threatened with change—an overwhelming concept after centuries of isolation. Suddenly, people were faced with new Western ideas: representative government, beer, foreign trade, and even eating meat. The leaders of the day were determined to have the West regard Japanese as equals—not as a tribe of strange-looking people with quaint or inexplicable social customs.

Imagine the shock to a foreign visitor arriving at the door of a *ryokan*, only to be told that he had to remove his shoes. After stepping onto tatami mats in a paper-walled room, he would be expected to change into a kimono. The only furniture in the room, aside from a cupboard for clothes and bedding, and a low table, was a dressing table with no legs—he would have to sit on the floor to use it. The only mirror in the room was covered with a silk curtain to prevent intrusive reflections.

He would be shown into a larger room: his bedroom, dining room, and living room all in one. In accordance with Japanese tradition, there was an alcove (*tokonoma*) with a hanging scroll and a flower arrangement beneath it, a table with no legs to be used as a desk, and a slightly higher dining table to sit beside on a flat brocade cushion.

In order to use the lavatory, he would be expected to change into bathroom slippers

The Rokumeikan. (Courtesy of the Architectural Institute of Japan)

and then squat over a hole in the floor. To take a bath, he would be required to soap and rinse clean *before* getting into the tub that he was to share with other guests. Dinner was taken back in his room, alone. The meal consisted of many small courses, including raw fish that he was meant to appreciate for its appearance and texture on the tongue, not solely for its taste. Coffee was unknown, tea was green, and there was no dessert. After dinner, the table was removed and a *futon* mattress and small hard pillow were put on the floor.

Imperial Japan needed a hotel.

It needed an imperial hotel, a showcase in which visitors from abroad could see how far Japan had progressed beyond its feudal origins. The entire staff would have to speak English. There would have to be a Continental menu. Chairs. Tables. Beds. In a daring break with tradition, guests would neither be expected to dine alone in their rooms nor bathe together in a communal tub. An imperial hotel would signal to the world that Japan had entered the modern age.

The Meiji Restoration had been a revolution by one ruling class against another. The dual system in which the emperor was merely a titular head while all power was in the hands of the shogunate had come to an end. After having overthrown a feudal system that was strangling the economy, thereby rousing the nation from its sleep of isolation, the Meiji government now had to face an equally difficult challenge. National prestige demanded that the country greet its Western guests with Western hospitality.

Kaoru Inoue, Minister of Foreign Affairs, had received a Western education in England. He was convinced that in order to revise unfavorable trade agreements that had been made with Europe and America, Japan would have to negotiate as an equal and meet the West on its own terms. Keenly aware of the need to provide dignitaries with accommodations more suited to their customs and preferences, he called together a group of prominent businessmen, people who had the most to gain by increased trade with the West. He argued that a hotel was more than a business venture, it was an investment in the nation's future, a backdrop against which Japan could enter the twentieth century.

Enter Baron Okura.

A concept of peerage based on the European system was initiated to placate former feudal lords stripped of their daimyo

Kaoru Inoue.
(Courtesy of Kyodo Tsushin)

Kihachiro Okura.

Eiichi Shibusawa. (Courtesy of Shibusawa Memorial Museum)

status. It was also flexible enough to include wealthy merchants who had made large contributions to the new administration. Almost overnight, Kihachiro Okura had amassed a fortune selling weapons to the government for its modern army. Okura (whose construction company built the Rokumeikan), Viscount Shibusawa, and Baron Iwasaki were members of the private sector who met with Foreign Minister Inoue and members of the Imperial Household Ministry in order to solve the government's embarrassment at not having a large, comfortable Western-style hotel in Tokyo at a time when Japan was encouraging travel from abroad. The ministry (today called the Imperial Household Agency) was responsible for the personal, ceremonial, and official affairs of the emperor and his family. Its contribution of ¥50,000 made it the single largest shareholder in the newly formed Imperial Hotel Limited Company. The balance of capital funding, an additional ¥210,000, was raised from other members of the group, who then leased 25,000 square feet of land in Ginza. The parcel of land was just across from Hibiya Park and not far from the Imperial Palace.

A German firm (Ende, Bockman and Company) that had been invited to Japan to design buildings for the Meiji government drew up plans for the new hotel. This was part of the "look to the West" philosophy that brought in British engineers for road systems (which is why traffic in Japan is on the left).

Construction of the Imperial Hotel began in January 1888. The site selected was on landfill that had been the Hibiya inlet of Tokyo Bay, the same site on which the Imperial Tower stands today. However, the original developers became concerned that the ground might prove too soft to support a foundation strong enough to withstand the weight of the building. Then there were second thoughts about the design. All of which was quite understandable: the Imperial Hotel had not been conceived as a purely commercial venture.

The first Imperial Hotel. (Courtesy of Shibusawa Memorial Museum)

With national prestige and pride at stake, a Japanese architect was called in.

Yuzuru Watanabe was an engineer with the Ministry of Internal Affairs. He had been to Germany and had studied its architecture. The perfect middleman, Watanabe could be trusted to be sympathetic to his countrymen's needs while dealing with Ende, Bockman and Company. Unfortunately, since the foundation was nearly completed by the time he took charge, it was impossible for him to exert free rein over the design. Rather than being the Japanese vision of what a Westerner would want, the hotel was a German version of the Japanese vision of what a Westerner would want.

The three-story wood-frame building faced in brick was an oddly eclectic Italianate structure that immediately became the talk of the town. It had mansard roofing, intricate wrought-iron balustrades, and arched balconies supported by fluted columns with Ionic capitals. There was a horseshoe-shaped driveway from the two front gates that ran past a front garden protecting the entrance from view. Inside were 70 guest rooms: high-ceilinged, spacious apartments with wood-burning fireplaces, ornate wood paneling, and massive pieces of furniture. There were beautiful murals *à la Japonaise* with whimsical natural scenery, and in the lounges, hundreds of painted butterflies appeared to flutter around the ceiling fixtures.

Beds were imported from the United States, wines from France, linens from Ireland, and silver from Britain. There was a ballroom described in a local newspaper at the time as "spacious, lofty, beautifully proportioned, handsomely decorated, the arrangement for music quite exceptional and the floor ideally perfect for dancing."

The lounge of the first Imperial Hotel. Note the painted ceilings and walls.

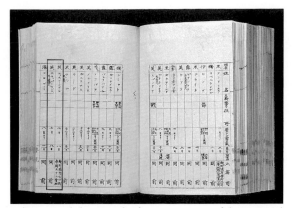

Police record showing the first two guests of the Imperial Hotel—Mr. Moore and Mr. Perkins. (Courtesy of the Tokyo Metropolitan Archives)

There was also a dining room, a lounge in which to read newspapers, a billiard room, and a concert hall. But what fascinated most Japanese was that the dining room served beef and pork, foods discouraged by Buddhist teachings in Japan and previously available only in places that catered exclusively to foreigners.

The Imperial Hotel opened on November 3, 1890, the Meiji emperor's birthday. Sometime prior to that, the Tokyo *Nichi Nichi* newspaper commented on the vogue for adding the word "Imperial" to the names of schools, buildings, insurance companies, and even fishing boats. Cynically, they wondered what people would do if a porter carried a bucket on which "Imperial Toilet Cleaning" was written.

The sarcasm was short-lived. It was the Tokyo *Nichi Nichi* itself that said of the new venture "The Imperial Hotel is beyond words." Acclaiming it as one of the most beautiful hotels in the world, the paper concluded that the nation had solved its problem in dealing with foreign visitors. "We have everything we need in the capital."

Except for one thing.

On opening day, amid the flush of success over the completion of a farsighted joint venture between government and industry designed to alleviate a matter of intense national concern, the Imperial Hotel at 1, Uchi-Yamashita-cho, Koji-machi-ku, Tokyo, had only two guests: a Mr. H. R. Moore and a Mr. M. Perkins.

They were to have the butterflies all to themselves.

The Imperial Hotel had fewer than 600 guests during the first six months after its opening. Able to accommodate over 100 people per night, reservations averaged a paltry 14. On most evenings only about 15 dinners were served in the cavernous dining room. This daringly conceived grand hotel, the most modern and expensive in the nation, sat poised and waiting to be discovered—as did Japan itself.

The fact that manager M. Yokoyama was able to keep the doors open while operat-

Advertisement for the Hotel Metropole, circa 1905. (Courtesy of Yushodo)

ing deeply in the red was due to the patronage of the Imperial Household Ministry. In a decade in which any purely commercial enterprise would have gone out of business, the Imperial played host to the House of Peers after the Diet building burned down. The ballroom was turned into an assembly hall, and plush rooms that had been designed to make foreign visitors feel comfortable were used as offices.

At the end of the Sino-Japanese War in 1895, occupancy averaged an all-time high of only 31 guests a day; this was mainly as the result of a trade fair that attracted businessmen eager to sell ships, railroads, and textile mills to the victorious Japanese.

The U.S. annexation of the Philippines in 1902 brought the first steady stream of American tourists, who added a Tokyo stopover to their trip to Manila. However, it wasn't until after another war—this one with Russia in 1905—that Japan finally attracted worldwide attention and more visitors than it could handle. A rise in the number of tours to Asia brought an ever-increasing number of guests to the hotel— as did completion of the Trans-Siberian railway that linked Europe with the Orient. Despite a shockingly expensive (at the time) room rate of three to five yen per night, and two to three yen for a Western-style lunch or dinner, the Imperial was filled to capacity and often had to turn away business.

Emil Flaig, the German who managed the Imperial at this time, initiated plans to build an annex. Eventually the Metropole, a smaller hotel, would be taken over to meet the increasing need for Western-style accommodations. At last, the world had validated the predictions of the Imperial's Meiji-era founders.

So, too, had Japan. Magazine articles and government memos reflected concern about appropriate lodgings for foreigners.

Japanese business leaders acknowledged the importance of a favorable national image not only as a means for increasing tourism, but for international business as well. Western-style construction was booming in Tokyo: there were even buildings with names that included the English-language word "building." A Japan Tourist Bureau was established and it was decided, in order to house the expected increase in visitors, to build a new and bigger Imperial Hotel.

However, Japan would have to wait once again for the world to set its watches to Tokyo time: the outbreak of World War I brought tourism to a virtual halt.

Imperial Hotel postcard, featuring a photo of the hotel's facade, the system of bridges leading to the Imperial Palace, and Mt. Fuji. Circa 1900.

The Second Imperial

There are conflicting reports on how American architect Frank Lloyd Wright was selected to create plans for the new Imperial. Reading his autobiography, one has the impression that Wright made a trip to Japan in 1913 at the invitation of the emperor after a committee had scoured the world for the best architect. However, Brendan Gill, in his biography of Wright (*Many Masks: A Life of Frank Lloyd Wright*), raises the possibility that Wright made the trip primarily to purchase Japanese woodblock prints for sale to American collectors (a highly profitable enterprise that supplemented his income between design fees). When approached by the emperor's representatives, Wright drew upon his personal charisma and established reputation within the architectural community to secure the commission. Another scenario is found in an article written by Wright-scholar Kathryn Smith: She states that a prominent Chicago banker who shared Wright's interest in Oriental art recommended him to Aisaku Hayashi, the hotel's general manager.

No matter how the commission began (whether accuracy depends merely on a correct sequence of events, or as in *Rashomon,* on who is telling the story) the fact remains that hiring Wright in 1916 was as astute a choice as building a Western-style hotel had been in 1890. The directors of the Imperial Hotel accomplished, with this single commission, what politics and economics had not been able to do. In a bold and brilliant stroke, they succeeded in turning all eyes East.

Wright embarked on the Imperial project estimating that it would take two years and net a generous fee (for 1916) of $40–50,000. Instead, it took six years and rewarded him far more handsomely: Despite all his prior successes and accolades within the architectural community, it was the Imperial Hotel that made him world famous.

Wright was a complex man with a turbulent personal life. Although married, he lived with another woman, who accompanied him to Tokyo; he fell ill repeatedly, succumbing most often, it has been suggested, to his own emotional stress; he battled the inner conflict between an engineer's need for precision and an artist's need for freedom. But his most severe adversary, the one with whom he would have the battle royal of his career—and win—was Nature herself.

The most important question was how to build the Imperial so that it could survive a major earthquake. That is what Hayashi wanted to know when he met with Wright in a Chicago restaurant. The architect pointed to a waiter carrying a tray of dishes balanced on the extended palm of one hand and explained that he would use the principle of the cantilever, the balanced load. A series of nine-foot-wide concrete pins would reach down into the muddy landfill and the building would "float" on them—like the waiter's tray.

The plan was to have breaks or joints in the building at least every 60 feet that would allow sections to rise and fall independently of one another. Flexibility was to be its strength. Floors were supported at the center and not where they met the walls, since walls might move in a quake. Pipes and wires were strung loosely so as not to snap or pull apart. Windows were designed in small sections. Wright disguised an enormous reservoir as an elegant lotus pond in front of the main entrance: the fires that followed huge earthquakes were known to cause more damage than the quakes themselves. The roof was to be made of lightweight copper so that a collapse would not bring the rest of the building with it or cause a shower of roof tiles that could prove fatal. Wright referred to the Imperial Hotel as the first building designed to be pushed and pulled. "Why fight the quake?" he asked. "Why not sympathize with it and outwit it?"

That he did. While others have claimed that the concept of pins (waiter's fingers) never worked and that Wright settled for an immense concrete slab resting on mud, the irony is that the Imperial did survive Tokyo's greatest earthquake—but very nearly did not survive its greatest architect.

Wright arrived in Japan in November of 1918. It was anticipated that the hotel would cost nearly three million yen, and completion was planned for the fall of 1920. The site itself became a series of giant workshops for stone cutting, roof tiles, and furnishings. Everything had to be perfect. According to Wright's vision. No matter that Japanese builders tried to dissuade him from using oya, a locally available porous stone. No matter that the Imperial's board of directors was concerned about having so ordinary a material as stucco-like volcanic tuff serve as the official countenance for a hotel that was to be a symbol of Japanese prominence in the world. As it turned out, the builders were correct in their concern; the directors, however, had no cause for alarm. Nothing about the Imperial would ever be ordinary.

The "Form follows function" motto of Wright's mentor, Louis H. Sullivan, was expanded into the even more demanding concept that form and function were one. Wright strived for a unity in which decoration was unique and indigenous to architecture. The deep eaves, decorative elements, and interpenetrating spaces that are so representative of his organic architectural style were never more fabulously pre-

sented than at the Imperial. Cary James, in his book *The Imperial Hotel*, describes it as "the frustration of spaces which demand the effort of involvement . . . half-seen vistas, always eye and body are drawn through and up and beyond."

Wright was responsible not only for the architectural plans but for a total, unified design that included all decoration—the furniture, floor and wall coverings, lighting and china. His unique vision alone defined every aspect of a hotel that was supposed to be "Western-style" but which was, in fact, unlike anything the West had ever seen. Nor was it like anything the Orient had ever seen. Imagine trying to describe the difference between red and green to a blind person. Wright's personal definitions offered no easy translation into the vernacular then or now: the Imperial resembled nothing but itself.

The outer shell was a mosaic of brick and oya that hugged the earth in a three-story horizontal shape similar to a capital letter H bisected at the crossbar with a capital letter I. There were large garden courts surrounding the hotel. Its richly ornamented facade was made possible because the oya stone could be carved so easily. Wright recalled in his autobiography that "We had a hundred or more clever stone 'choppers' beating out patterns of the building on the greenish, leopard-spotted lava . . ." There were some 600 workers and their families living on the site. "And we tried faithfully—sometimes frantically and often profanely—to teach them how to build it, half-way between our way and their way . . . How skillful they were! What craftsmen! How patient and clever."

However, it soon became apparent that neither the completion date nor the budget would be met. Costs were on their way to doubling. Further, there was the unspoken concern that Wright's devotion to perfection bordered on the eccentric, as did his behavior in living with a woman who was not his wife. Wright's demand for perfection prolonged a construction period that would have been difficult for the board to justify under the best of circumstances: The hotel-in-progress, with its workers living on site, and all the noise and confusion of such an enterprise, proved a major upset for guests in the 1890 building right next door. The management could not offer the tranquil setting they felt obliged to provide. Predictably, Wright refused to compromise his design in order to lower costs and speed up construction.

On April 16, 1922, the original Imperial Hotel burned to the ground. All that remained was an adjoining undistinguished structure that Wright had built earlier to replace the old Imperial's annex. The board of directors was at the helm of a non-existent business. On one side was rubble from the fire. On the other, rubble from the construction. The Imperial Hotel was unable to offer accommodations or services. Or excuses.

The directors, in a remarkable act of contrition over the death of one guest in the fire, accepted full responsibility for the loss and resigned. Wright, no longer able to count on his two staunchest supporters (Okura and Hayashi were among those leaving), revised his schedule and promised to open the north wing and central section within a few months.

The new manager, H.K.S. Yamaguchi, gave Wright full credit for meeting the new deadline. With a number of public rooms and the south wing (a duplicate of the north) yet to be finished, Wright's assistant, Arata Endo, was put in charge. Wright left for home. He would never see his vision completed and he would never return to Japan.

Antonin Raymond, the architect who became Wright's protégé and worked closely with him, claims that Wright was fired before the building was finished and that that was the reason for his departure. Kathryn Smith reports that Wright was not fired, that he left after a number of tributes and ceremonies in his honor.

According to the Imperial, Wright *was* fired, both for coming in late and going over budget on a project that had tripled its original estimate to finally reach a high of some nine million yen. By the time the hotel was built, Wright said with a smile that he knew they had spent a great deal on the hotel, but the good news was that they wouldn't have to buy any paintings.

Although still unfinished when the public was allowed in, the Imperial had instant celebrity, drawing as many sightseers as the traditional tourist spots in Tokyo. Visiting Americans thought the reason the structure looked strange to them was because Wright had designed a Japanese-style hotel. Others saw a Mayan or Aztec influence. Still others claimed that Wright had recycled his plans for a South American project that had fallen through. In fact, Wright was not one to build Mayan, or Aztec, or even Japanese: there was not a single Japanese design element to be found in the hotel. If anything, the plans for the Imperial resembled more closely those for an American property he had designed—the Midway Gardens. The most he could be accused of was building *for* the Japanese but, far more accurately, Wright built for Wright. Brendan Gill says, "The hotel had no more to do with Japan than it did with Colonial New England, and if the Japanese took pride in it at all, it was on account of its strangeness. Like Midway Gardens, the building was a freak, the offspring of genius."

Wright had designed the main entrance to be dignified and exclusive. He had per-

The second Imperial Hotel, designed by Frank Lloyd Wright.

Detail of the decorative effects in the Peacock Room. Note the hexagonal-back chairs.

ceived the hotel as serving a small number of select guests. Indeed, every person who came to the Imperial for a banquet was escorted by a staff member to the banquet room. To enter the Imperial Hotel was an event.

The Japanese were not yet devotees of "hotel hopping" or meeting in lobby lounges for some coffee and a chat. Indeed, from the outside there was no way to see the lobby: steps went down and then up again almost as a deterrent to traffic from the street.

The degree to which the Imperial was outside the social ken of local Japanese was most apparent when farmers, passing the striking facade and wary of what lay within, would stop to throw coins in the pool for good luck.

While the basic architectural plan was simple—or at least symmetrical—the intricate detail that had been lavished on it contributed an atmosphere of mystery. The interior spaces were as highly ornamental as the facade. Wright had designed distinctive furniture throughout: hexagonal-backed chairs that harmonized with hexagonal-shaped cornices and ceilings. Fabrics and rugs were based on a design of discs and overlapping circles. Carved oya stone was everywhere, often catching threads from dresses or suits as people passed by.

Lounges were located on either side of the lobby and were accessible only by narrow, winding staircases. All luggage and packages had to be carried by hand: there were too many stairs for bellmen to use carts or trolleys—even for room service. The swimming pool in the basement had no windows and could not be ventilated properly. The oya stone walls absorbed the moisture, making it a very dank place. At the very least, the Imperial offered its guests an unforgettably exotic adventure.

In one of the great ironies of history, a few moments before a luncheon celebrating the formal opening of the hotel on September 1, 1923, Tokyo experienced the most powerful earthquake in its history. The Great Kanto Earthquake destroyed most of Tokyo and Yokohama.

Except for the Imperial Hotel. It rode the quake like a ship at sea.

One of the earliest messages out of Tokyo was a cable from Baron Okura to Wright. It said, HOTEL STANDS UNDAMAGED AS MONUMENT OF YOUR GENIUS! HUNDREDS OF HOMELESS PROVIDED BY PERFECTLY MAINTAINED SERVICE! CONGRATULATIONS.

A stunning eyewitness report of what had happened was recorded by Tetsuzo Inumaru, who had been appointed general manager a few months earlier. Inumaru, who had worked with Wright on the design of the kitchen, wrote his account three months later. It remains an extraordinary document.

"At the time of the earthquake I was in my office. When the building began to shake, I ran to the kitchen, knowing this was the first place fire was most likely to break out. I found the electric cooking ranges toppled and aflame from fat that had ignited, and fire spreading in every direction. I sent a boy to the hotel's power station and our engineer managed to cut off the current not only to the kitchen but to the entire building.

"We extinguished the fires before they reached the kitchen ceiling, which fortunately was very high, and before the walls caught fire. While I was on the steps coming up from the kitchen, a second sharp quake occurred, but I knew that the hotel was safe from fires starting within.

"Following the second quake, I was making my way to the banquet hall when I met Arata Endo, who had helped Frank

Lobby of the second Imperial Hotel.

Lloyd Wright in the construction of the hotel. We went to the hall together, and were there when the third shock hit the building. It was severe—just like being in a storm at sea. We knew it was no use thinking about getting out of a window, so we stood in the center of the room while electric fans were dislodged and falling from the balconies around us. Our own annex—a temporary building in which we had stopped housing guests—had collapsed.

"Emergency fire-fighters wet down the building as best they could, using the pond water in front of the hotel and the running water outside. We could see sparks and flashes from the burning buildings across the street, because the electric switches had not been turned off.

"That first night the danger came from the quake-ignited fires. The second night brought a scare concerning possible 'invasion' of the hotel by raiders. Thousands of refugees had congregated in Hibiya Park, opposite the hotel and just across the street. What would they do if they could not get food—or if it should rain? The Imperial Hotel, standing so magnificently unscathed amid the ruins of Tokyo, was in a dangerous position.

"The day following the earthquake there were some disorders and raiding in the city, and wild rumors began to circulate of large bands of looters on the march. A Japanese official advised me confidentially that these bands might head for the Imperial Hotel—now the diplomatic and commercial center of the striken city—to cut all communications. With several ambassadors in residence and many other foreign guests, the need to take special precautions was obvious. The entire hotel staff armed themselves with whatever defensive weapons they could find and mounted guard throughout that second night.

"At the time of the earthquake at noon on September 1, 1923, there were ninety-three guests registered in the hotel. A few hours later there were three times as many staying in the Imperial and hundreds more coming in and out, with resultant wild confusion. I set up my office outside the front entrance and there it remained through three climactic weeks. The embassies organized relief work, handled by many volunteer workers besides the staffs, and the hotel became a combined information bureau and relief center for the entire community. Guests and refugees all spent the nights either sitting outside in the front court or in the lobby, or lying on mattresses spread out in the inner court on the grass. For a week no one slept in the guest rooms as aftershocks continued to shake the building.

"The Imperial Hotel had no water supply, no lights, no usable stoves, and no telephone operating. No trains or cars were running; no telegrams could be sent. As for water, most fortunately an outside hydrant adjacent to the hotel kitchen never gave out, so we made our campfire there for cooking. Another outside hydrant was used by all hotel guests for washing. Refugees from Hibiya Park filled their buckets at the latter or from another hydrant in the street beside the hotel, and at night, after dark, some took baths there."

The new Imperial Hotel—so daringly designed by Frank Lloyd Wright as an elegant setting for international diplomacy, financial intrigue, and high-society glamour—began its career as a refuge for thousands left homeless and desolate by the Great Kanto Earthquake. The hotel's reputation was enhanced further by the fantasy that it was the only building left standing in Tokyo. Such was not the case: dozens of buildings remained intact. But the world press picked up on the drama of Baron Okura's cable to Wright and accorded the

Imperial perhaps its only unearned touch of flamboyance.

The kitchen facilities designed by general manager Tetsuzo Inumaru were among the largest available in downtown Tokyo, as was the water supply provided by the lotus-pad—covered reservoir upon which Wright had insisted. These two factors made the Imperial a logical choice as central headquarters for the hungry and displaced.

Ironically, it also became headquarters for the diplomats whose embassies had been destroyed, and the international corps of reporters and photographers sent to cover the earthquake's devastation. The Imperial Hotel was featured in almost every story to come out of Tokyo. Under happier conditions it would have been a press agent's dream. The Imperial had in residence, virtually within hours of its opening, precisely the people it had hoped to attract, as well as those who controlled the media. A news-hungry world would learn that the Imperial (quite literally) was "the only place to be."

Months later, after Wright had been accorded worldwide fame for having built the hotel that survived the great quake, he was to fill out a questionnaire for his inclusion in *Who's Who in America*. Kathryn Smith notes that in responding to the question "What have you done that is worthy of special mention?" he replied, "The Imperial Hotel of Tokyo, Japan and 176 other Buildings of Note."

Much of the credit for the Imperial's responsiveness to its guests and staff, as well as to the needy of Tokyo during the chaotic post-quake period, goes to its general manager, Tetsuzo Inumaru. His consummate professionalism and sensitivity were matched perfectly to the requirements of his chosen field. What makes his story all the more interesting is that he

Tetsuzo Inumaru.

grew up to become something that had never before existed in his country. With no role models to follow, and only his instincts, determination, and inner strength to guide him, a middle-class Japanese farmer's son became one of the world's leading hoteliers.

After graduating in 1910 from what is now Hitotsubashi University (the alma mater of many Japanese financiers and industrialists), Inumaru decided that he wanted to be in the hotel business. Knowing that he would have to start at the bottom, the college graduate worked as a hotel cook, first in Manchuria and then in Shanghai. While his Hitotsubashi classmates sought prominent positions in government or high-paying jobs in industry, they tried to convince him that it was a disgrace to their school to have one of its graduates work as a common cook. But Inumaru was determined to learn the hotel business from the kitchen up. His friends then offered to finance the opening of his own hotel. No. Inumaru was also stubborn. Assuming that if he knew how to cook he could at least earn a living, Inumaru set sail for Europe—birthplace of the grand hotel.

He arrived in London with high hopes and four pounds in his pocket. Parlaying one job into another, he soon accumulated enough experience and good references to be hired by Claridge's—despite lacking the requisite apprenticeship in a French kitchen. From Claridge's, he went on to the Ritz in Paris and finally to the Waldorf-Astoria in New York. Inumaru referred to the nine-year apprenticeship during which he turned his back on a comfortable business career at home as "the years I invested to learn luxury."

They paid off. In 1920, after handling almost every aspect of the hotel business, he was offered a position as an assistant manager at the new Imperial Hotel that Frank Lloyd Wright was building. Since Wright was unfamiliar with the technical layout of a hotel kitchen, and Inumaru was a Japanese who had worked in the Waldorf's state-of-the-art kitchen, he was seen as a promising candidate to help bring the new hotel to fruition. Equally impressive credentials were his ironbound rule of "one person, one duty" and a decision to greet guests with a sense of gratitude for their patronage.

But Inumaru, like César Ritz himself, had to invent the environment in which his talents would eventually flourish. Not only did he have to learn the hotel business, but he had to redesign it. In so doing, Tetsuzo Inumaru created the benchmark against which all other hotels in Japan would be measured for decades to come.

The first months of the Wright Imperial were blessedly less turbulent than its open-ing day. Within weeks, Tokyo had begun to rebuild. While charity banquets held at the Imperial raised funds for earthquake relief, guests at the hotel allowed themselves to enjoy the luxury and romance of Wright's design. A second quake in January of 1924, only half as severe as the Kanto disaster, did no damage to the hotel apart from the reappearance of some large cracks that had been repaired from the earlier shake. While the rest of Tokyo once again experienced chimneys and walls crashing down around them that year, the Imperial played host to 23,000 resident guests as well as more than 150,000 people in the dining room and grill.

The Imperial quickly became the social center of Tokyo, the favorite gathering place for foreign diplomats, guests, and their Japanese friends. Saturday-night dinner-dances were among the most popular events in town. As such, they became the target for a demonstration by ultra-rightists later in 1924, urging management to stop holding the Western dances which they termed a demoralizing and harmful influence on national morale. Entering the main dining room of the hotel, some forty *soshi* (rightists) proceeded to leap onstage, draw their weapons as menacingly as possible, and perform a traditional sword dance, hoping to intimidate both Japanese and foreign guests.

Tetsuzo Inumaru came to the rescue by ordering the orchestra to play the national anthem. The "super-patriots" stood at attention, confused. They shouted three *banzai* for the Emperor and departed. Having avoided a confrontation that might have erupted into violence, Inumaru—a firm believer that a hotel's first responsibility is the safety of its guests—discontinued the Saturday-night dances. He noted that during a period in which the government had a policy toward frugality, "dancing was considered by the majority of the Japanese as being a pastime of the wealthy."

On a lighter note, the Japanese didn't mind *all* the pastimes of the wealthy. When it was learned that the Graf Zeppelin would stop in Tokyo, *The Japan Times*, an English-language paper, carried front-page stories for nearly the entire month of August 1929 that chronicled each breeze en route. All this despite the fact that it cost each passenger, most of whom were not, however, Japanese, some $9000 to make the around-the-world trip.

One headline read:

SUKIYAKI WILL BE SERVED ON
    ZEPPELIN;
Imperial Hotel to Prepare Food Taken
    Across the Pacific

The Imperial had been named caterer for the six-day flight from Tokyo to Los Angeles and would provide 1098 meals "of the best grade" for 40 crew and 21 passengers making the trip. The newspaper reported that "No two same dishes will be seen on the dinner table throughout the trip, for the Zeppelin features [the Imperial Hotel's] excellent food."

Since the trip was made at the height of summer, and the airship's refrigeration system could store food for only three days, additional provisions were put into cans and packed in dry ice. The challenge was, of course, to prepare non-perishable dishes worthy of so lofty a venture. All of which makes one question whether the foremost French kitchen in Japan actually did serve sukiyaki.

No matter. The zeppelin had captured the imagination of the world. Its arrival and departure made headlines and, as always, so did the Imperial. By now, the hotel's image was linked to international events and front-page news. The future seemed more secure and brighter than ever as the hotel anticipated plans for a Japanese

THE GRAF ZEPPELIN
OVER TOKYO
THE IMPERIAL HOTEL

Cover of the Zeppelin menu. The Imperial catered the food served on the Pacific portion of the trip.

world's fair to be held in 1939, and a Tokyo Olympic Games in 1940. But the Imperial had not anticipated war.

By 1945, thirty percent of Japan was homeless. The Japanese people had suffered three million casualties. The country's economy was in ruins. Japan had lost more than a war, it had lost an empire. The Japanese, who had never heard their emperor speak, were shocked by the very sound of his voice, no less than by his words informing them that they must accept total surrender and "endure the unendurable." They responded according to a long tradition of obedience to authority. The nation that had once forbidden foreigners on their shores prepared to accept an occupation of their homeland that would last for nearly seven years.

The man designated to rule Japan was

General Douglas A. MacArthur, Supreme Commander of the Allied Powers. During the period of occupation, the Japanese government was to carry out his orders.

Japanese Foreign Minister Mamoru Shigemitsu was staying at the Imperial. In her memoirs, Imperial housekeeper Toshiko Takeya recalls the period after the war. "It was an exceptionally hot summer. The heat continued day after day. Even as we entered autumn (normally a time of typhoons and evening storms) there was no hint of rain. Shigemitsu was staying in adjoining rooms 244 and 248. Every morning he'd leave early and return late, drenched in sweat.

"I didn't know what would happen to our defeated country, but Shigemitsu was in the thick of the turmoil surrounding the talks about the terms of Japan's surrender. I hardly spoke to him except to say good morning and similar brief greetings . . . He started to look sterner and sterner, which made me worry about the direction of events for our defeated nation.

"Fuel was hard to come by in those days, and by the time Shigemitsu returned there was often no hot water left . . . I thought that even if he couldn't have a proper hot bath, warm water would be better to cleanse him of the sweat than cold, so I would bring warm water up from the kitchen. It took about eight trips to fill the bath with enough water to be useful . . . I used to do this before I returned home and it was probably for my own peace of mind more than his.

"Japan signed the formal document of surrender on the USS *Missouri* on September 2, 1945. Shigemitsu was invested with full plenipotentiary powers and he, with Chief of General Staff Umezu, was charged with the duty of representing Japan. The preceding evening, Shigemitsu asked me to help him in the morning because he had to be up early. I was on duty that night, and at four I took a cup of tea to Shigemitsu's room.

"When he was fully dressed, he seated himself formally on a chair and on colored paper (*washi*) composed a poem. I think he wrote on three pieces of paper. He gave one to me.

> *My life, rendered meaningless,*
> *Has been made worthwhile again*
> *Today is the day*
> *I shall become*
> *My country's shield.*

"Manager Inumaru and I ushered Shigemitsu to the hotel's entrance and bowed as he left."

During the war, Tetsuzo Inumaru had been instructed to run the Imperial as a center for foreign nationals in Japan, and the Axis powers and neutral diplomats set up their chancelleries in the hotel. As the fighting intensified, the number of foreigners declined and the hotel was frequented mainly by Japanese government officials. The minister of agriculture asked Inumaru to create a special wartime hotel organization to supervise the distribution of food quotas. His efforts made it possible to operate with near-normal menus and service even after the south wing of the hotel suffered damage in a firebombing raid.

As soon as the war was over, Inumaru was again required to host top American guests. Given the job of restaffing the American embassy in preparation for General MacArthur's arrival, he was responsible for everything from tableware to towels as well as recruiting skilled cooks and maids. Because there were no chairs or tables left in the embassy, he offered furniture from the hotel.

MacArthur planned to hold a reception at the Imperial for high-ranking American military officers. Inumaru recalled that when the general's car appeared at the front entrance of the hotel, "I was in the line waiting to receive him. Actually, I was at his command as a citizen of a defeated country." MacArthur asked Inumaru for a tour of the hotel. Then, finding that forty minutes still remained before the luncheon was to begin, he asked the hotelier to show him around Tokyo.

According to Hessell Tiltman, correspondent for *The Manchester Guardian*, longtime resident of the Imperial, and author of *The Imperial Hotel Story*, Inumaru was quoted as saying later that he felt Japan had been "very lucky" to have had MacArthur as supreme commander. "Many Japanese generals made triumphant entries into cities their forces had conquered but none of them made a sightseeing tour accompanied by a civilian of an enemy country. That General MacArthur did so indicated that he was indeed a great statesman."

The Imperial was requisitioned by the United States government as a prestige billet and meeting place for top officers and officials of MacArthur's GHQ, and to accommodate the supreme commander's guests. Rather than being disheartened by a switch in clientele from high-ranking Japanese to high-ranking Americans, Inumaru called the staff together and asked for their cooperation in providing the same quality of service to the Occupation Forces as they had traditionally provided prewar guests. He added that the staff had been given an unprecedented opportunity to study the likes and dislikes of foreign guests, and that they should seize the opportunity to improve their knowledge of how to run an international hotel more efficiently. "It is as if you went overseas to study."

One of Inumaru's priorities had to do with sanitation. He recalled that when the

Wright Imperial first opened, he had been responsible for making the kitchen a model of cleanliness. However, the Occupation Forces practiced even stricter standards. Inumaru also credited them with teaching the concept of fire prevention. "In Japan, our custom is to have water for fire-fighting available before retiring...should a fire break out. The Americans, we discovered, have another way of thinking—to prevent fire rather than extinguish a blaze."

But one blaze that could not be prevented came from Kishichiro Okura. Son of the founder of the original Imperial, the man who had sent Frank Lloyd Wright the post-quake cable that became so famous, Okura was president of the hotel at the time of Japan's surrender. No sooner had the U.S. Army taken over the hotel than he was dismissed from his post. As part of the purge of all Japanese corporate groups by GHQ, Okura was prohibited from conducting business of any kind.

It fell to Inumaru to tell his former boss that his presence at the Imperial was no longer welcome—obviously a difficult message to convey, since Okura had been his respected employer. The Okura family's incendiary response to that incident resulted in their eventually building their own hotel, brick by angry brick. Despite garbled press reports implying that Inumaru had driven Okura from the hotel, and the new Hotel Okura's flamboyantly competitive campaigns, it was Inumaru—not anyone from the rival hotel—who was the first to reach Okura's bedside when he died in 1963.

In November of 1945, an American, Lt. Timothy Morris, was assigned by GHQ to manage the hotel. Inumaru had a new boss. In his book, *The Wise Bamboo*, Morris describes his first sight of the hotel on the evening he arrived—wearing combat equipment, musette bag on his back, bayonet on his belt and carbine slung on his shoulder. "It was so dark that the building appeared to be just a large, black blotch. But then the moon came out from behind a cloud, brightening the lotus pond before the entrance into a shiny rectangle of silver and silhouetting the north and south wings so that they looked like two great claws projecting forward from the center dome of the building. My first impression of the Imperial Hotel was that it looked like a giant crab eating a stick of chewing gum with the tinfoil still on it."

As Morris recalls, the next morning, while he was taking a bath, "a pretty Japanese girl in a lovely kimono pushed the door open and started to walk into the room carrying my breakfast tray." Concerned about his lack of privacy, he took the matter up with Inumaru, whom he described as "a lively man in his late fifties, a mature ball of fire, short and compactly built and with a leonine cast to his features. His command of English was excellent though he spoke with an accent and in a staccato rhythm."

Inumaru explained that the maid's conduct was perfectly proper by Oriental standards and that the Japanese had a saying, "The nude is often seen but never looked at." Morris, who had no intention of being seen or looked at, immediately revised procedures by which staff entered rooms.

"The Imperial Hotel was in appalling condition," Morris writes. "The entire south wing had been gutted by incendiary bombs, the furnishings were worn threadbare, the employees' uniforms were tattered, the rooms and corridors needed repainting and most of the experienced members of the staff had fled Tokyo during the last days of the war in order to escape the B-29 raids." Yet, that was not the worst of it for Morris: He said that the

basic design of the Imperial, with its narrow corridors, steps, and inconveniently-placed service areas, made it a hotel manager's nightmare.

One can only imagine how extraordinarily difficult it must have been for Inumaru during this period to witness what he regarded as his hotel, in fact his life's work, being translated into the vernacular of the Occupation. Nowhere does one find a hint of melancholy or a note of complaint, but it would be hard to believe that he did not think back with crushing sadness to the Imperial's earlier grandeur, during the six and one-half years of Occupation while two million Allied personnel visited the hotel. In all that time, not one Japanese guest was admitted. With great diplomacy, Tetsuzo Inumaru summed up the experience by saying, "When they went home they spread word that it was a very good hotel. We are very grateful."

The Imperial was returned to its owners in March 1952, and opened for regular business six weeks before the sovereign independence of Japan was restored in accordance with the terms of the peace treaty. While the Occupation Forces had made some repairs, the real renovation and construction boom was about to begin. For the next eighteen years, until the new building opened in 1970, the Imperial was to go through a series of incarnations once again tied to the reshaping of Japan itself.

By 1954, the Imperial had repaired the damaged south wing and opened a new seven-story annex with 155 rooms. Next, the main building was renovated and air-conditioned. In 1956, plans were unveiled for a ten-story second annex. An additional 359 rooms would be available to handle a rise in tourism that was growing at a rate even faster than the fantastic upward spiral of the economy as a whole. One of the factors that gave tourism a boost was the inauguration of international air services linking Japan to the world. Prior to 1945, the Japanese government did not permit the routing of foreign aircraft within its borders.

But modernization of the Imperial was not to proceed without making nearly as much news as had its original construction. "Oh! No!" was the front-page headline reaction of Frank Lloyd Wright when shown photos of the new annex. By then eighty-nine years old (he would die the following year), Wright said, "I can't imagine a more outrageous insult to the feeling and character for the building, and for Japan . . . It's the most gosh awful thing to have done in Japan."

Japanese architect Teitaro Takahashi, who had designed the new building, responded to the criticism by calling Wright's creation a relic of the rickshaw age. "It's very nicely designed," Takahashi said, "but it's not at all Japanese—as he claims . . . the interior wastes a lot of space and is forbidding and uncomfortable . . . If Wright could see his building now, he'd probably reconsider the design." Takahashi went on to explain that it's "practically falling apart . . . The stone eaves have been falling off for the last three years . . . The whole center of the hotel is sinking."

Inumaru, by then president of the Imperial, said, "It's more than a matter of style. Wright designed the building when there were no automobiles, no air-conditioning, no traffic noises . . . We have to build more efficiently today." Questions of aesthetics were put aside as the hotel stood by its position that the old Imperial was uneconomical to run and not as safe as it used to be.

While reports concur that the hotel, a unique structure of shadow and light, was in need of massive renovation, it is impossible to overlook the additional fact that Japan was in the midst of seeking a new image for itself. It was an era during which almost anything new was better than anything old. And since no one had ever claimed that the old Imperial was old Japanese art, it lacked sufficient credentials to override the emotional and commercial priorities of a nation seeking to reestablish itself on its own terms. The Frank Lloyd Wright Imperial would survive only another decade.

The decision to hold the 1964 Olympic Games in Tokyo heralded a new era for postwar Japan: the world was welcoming the nation back into the global family. All eyes were focused on a country in the first flush of a brilliant recovery. Between 1960 and 1964 there was a construction boom in which the Japanese hotel industry came of age.

For the first time in its history, the Imperial had competitors. Although it had an unmatched tradition of service, it was no longer the only choice of hotel. Therefore, the Imperial knew it had to be the best choice. The hotel that had fashioned its kitchen after the Waldorf-Astoria, and its spirit and cuisine after the grand hotels of Europe, now began to draw on its own strengths: a purely Japanese style of management.

The turning point for the Imperial was its headline-making decision to raze the Wright building. After years of endless repairs, the hotel had no choice. According to the Imperial, Wright hadn't taken the climate into account and concentrated solely on anti-earthquake measures. They faulted the architect's insistence on using porous oya stone for the facade and interior spaces of the hotel. "The stone was spongy and soaked up the moisture. It began to crumble. You didn't know whether it was raining inside or out. The city Fire Department told us we couldn't operate as a hotel any longer in that building. The top was light, the beams were wood: every year we had to adjust the doors and windows. The building kept tilting." Postwar subway construction and the gradual drawing away of water on which the building once "floated" now caused it to sag dangerously.

The world press had a field day when the announcement was made. Devotees of the old Imperial were saddened and some were outraged—but no group was more concerned about the decision than the directors of the Imperial. Frank Lloyd Wright had been a rather heretical figure with little international reputation when commissioned to design the hotel. Some 60 years later, he was considered by many to be the most brilliant architect in the world. Although Wright's name had been linked inseparably with the Imperial, the hotel's directors took the more pragmatic position that it was neither Wright's fame nor his talent that had made the Imperial a great hotel.

Architects and historians immediately formed committees to protect Wright's Imperial, as a *New York Times* editorial wrote, from "falling victim to 'progress'." There were protests that the building must be saved as "an artistic treasure." The *Times* called it a "museum-like structure" and wondered in a flourish of naiveté "how the great American architect managed to combine so subtly the look of the Orient with his familiar geometric touches from the American Southwest."

Not everyone concurred with the *Times*. In a letter to the editors, British journalist Anthony West called it a "hideous and inconvenient building" with "neo-Aztec facades, all combined to make it a depressing eyesore." He wrote that Wright's "Aztec-moderne fantasy" was a "monstrosity" that would only stand as a "monument to a failure of understanding and communication."

Predictably, Mrs. Frank Lloyd Wright did not agree with West. The architect's widow flew to Tokyo, walked into her husband's hotel for the first time in her life— and immediately noticed that something was wrong. "You see those stone decorations in the front? Some of them have been taken away."

"I have all of the drawings and the old photographs of the hotel right here," Olgivanna Wright was quoted as saying while she tapped her forehead. On her way in, she stopped to remove a "Keep off the grass" sign. Then she looked down at the badly worn tan carpets. "They are still beautiful. They can be restored."

Mrs. Wright was determined to find a way to save the Imperial. "One of my proposals is that the hotel be moved brick by brick to another location in Tokyo." And that is, in fact, what was done eventually— at least for the main entrance and its immediate interior. They were moved to the Meiji Mura Museum in Inuyama, some 200 miles from Tokyo, although the oya stone proved so fragile that it had to be reconstructed. An outdoor museum with over 50 reproduced structures from the Meiji period, Meiji Mura provided a permanent home for the facade of the Wright building.

The Third Imperial

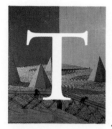The opening year of the 1970s saw the first of the 747 jumbo jets that would usher in a new era in travel. There had been over 350,000 visitors to Japan during the 1964 Olympics; the Osaka Exposition, with its theme of "Progress and Harmony for Mankind," brought in more than 850,000. Tokyo was in the midst of a building boom that redefined real estate as the currency against which all other investments were measured.

On March 10, 1970, for the third time in its history, a new Imperial Hotel rose on the site of the old moat surrounding the Imperial Palace. Although a bureaucratic lid was placed on the height of the building (17 stories aboveground, 3 below) because of its proximity to the palace, the hotel was unveiled as the largest in Asia—the new main building had been constructed at a cost then of 23.7 billion yen, the most ever invested in a hotel in the Far East.

Tetsuzo Inumaru, after a 51-year career at the Imperial, was at the helm of what he called in 1970 "the hotel of tomorrow". He said, in his opening-day message, that the new building had been planned "as an answer to the demands of the coming age of mass international travel." It had been designed according to architect Teitaro Takahashi's dictum that the structure express dignity and flexibility.

An article in *The New York Times* said that the new building "gives a feeling of almost overwhelming spaciousness. Corridors that might be the set of an Antonioni movie stretch seemingly to the horizon. The lobby . . . could hold at least one basketball court. Luxury as well as space is conveyed by the interior of the new hotel."

A cynic might say that the brilliant hotelier who is currently president of the Imperial Hotel began his career with three strikes against him:

(1) He had a very famous father
(2) His father was in the hotel business
(3) The hotel his father managed was the Imperial.

Named Hotelier of the Year in 1988 by the industry's most prestigious magazine, Ichiro Inumaru had to do far more than follow in his father's footsteps: He was called upon to lead the Imperial into a future that no one had envisioned.

Tetsuzo Inumaru managed the hotel from 1923 to 1970, perhaps the most dramatic period in the history of modern Japan. In the midst of earthquake, war, occupation, and economic revival, he proved that the Imperial could offer all services expected of a world-class hotel. It then became the responsibility of his son, Ichiro, to keep the Imperial competitive with—and in the forefront of—those Japanese hotels that had learned from its pioneering example.

The Imperial is a publicly held corporation with a 20-member board, of which twelve are hoteliers. The board meets monthly; the hoteliers meet each week to review present and future goals. The key theme echoed throughout the Imperial's corridors, boardrooms, guest rooms and restaurants is its link with—but not dependence upon—the past. Nowhere is the strength of that chain more impressive than in the office of its president.

Ichiro Inumaru, a man who is unusually adept at putting people at ease, looked back on the last five decades of the Imperial's history and said, "It's hard to believe we have come so far. For one thing, back then few of us could speak much English. I recall a foreign friend telling me he once called the hotel to talk to a guest, a Mr.

Lamos from Greece. Upon hearing the guest's name, the operator asked, 'Is that *L* as in Rome?' My quick-witted friend replied, 'No, it's *R* as in London.' He was put straight through to his party."

These days, Japan is a hot topic of conversation, be it in Wall Street boardrooms or on Hollywood soundstages. Japanese artists and writers, politicians, industrialists, and chefs have become prominent players in the global arena. Traffic to and from Tokyo is at an all-time high, creating a more sophisticated and demanding clientele than ever before. Those content merely to maintain the status quo, instead of redefining it, cannot survive. Unlike his father, who created a hotel acceptable to the West, Ichiro Inumaru's unique achievement was to open the Imperial to the Japanese.

One staff member recalls his first visit to the hotel: "My parents took me to Tokyo in 1963 when I was a kindergarten student. Arriving at Tokyo Station after a seven-hour trip from Kyoto, I heard the taxi driver say Wow! when we told him we were going to stay at the Imperial. The only Japanese I saw when we went in were behind the front desk. It made me nervous and I grabbed my mother's hand.

"There was an American teenager sitting in the lobby, eating a huge chocolate bar. I kept watching him and my mother whispered to me that American chocolate was bitter. I believed her until I went to the United States as an adult.

"I remember that when my father dialed the telephone in our room, the switchboard operator spoke to him in English. My father asked for someone who spoke Japanese. "I am Japanese," the surprised operator said—in Japanese.

The first thing Inumaru remembers about the Imperial from his childhood was the smell of cigars as he entered the lobby.

President Ichiro Inumaru.

As a very dapper young man about town he wanted to go into the import-export business, but soon found himself scrubbing toilets at the Imperial. His father had him work every station from housekeeping to the kitchen and, after majoring in economics at Keio University, sent him to Cornell University's School of Hotel Administration. While in college, he worked during the summer as a busboy at the Mark Hopkins Hotel in San Francisco.

Next, he applied for a job at the Waldorf-Astoria. But this was during the postwar period, when it was difficult for Japanese to get work in the U.S. Still, he was confident of his experience and background. Leaving the personnel office, he went to the front desk and booked himself a room. Then, under the guise of being a guest, he asked to see the personnel manager. Within a few moments, the manager realized he was speaking to the son of Tetsuzo Inumaru and arranged for an apprentice position, since he could not offer a paying job.

After working at the Waldorf, Ichiro Inumaru went back to work for his father in Tokyo as an executive assistant manager at the Imperial. He recalls that years ago the Imperial was dependent upon tourist business but today it is mainly business travelers and diplomats who frequent the hotel. "Tour groups generally go to other hotels not as well located. They have buses to travel around in and don't have to be in the center of town." The Imperial's business guests often return four to five times each year with an average stay of three days. They believe it is a powerful sales weapon to have the Imperial as their Tokyo address.

With a staff-to-room ratio of nearly two to one, the Imperial has "a multi-faceted training program devised to provide a level of service like that of our original operation." Inumaru notes, however, that "while high-technology systems have proven very efficient and useful, they have remained behind the human faces they support, and not vice versa.

"Our prevailing philosophy concentrates on managing this as a small hotel, with the highly personalized service of a Japanese inn." Even with an enviable staff-to-room ratio he realizes the difficulties in providing such service and smiles. "It takes a workaholic Japanese labor force to be able to do this."

Inumaru arrives at the hotel between seven-thirty and eight o'clock in the morning so that he has time for a few words with the night shift before they go off duty. Those words always begin with the same sentence: "Did anything happen?" Then he's off to his award-lined office on the mezzanine, where he personally opens and reads all letters from guests. Asked what's in the letters or who they're from, Inumaru smiles: "A good hotel never talks about its guests."

With his top executives, Hiroshi Fujii and Kiyohito Minoshima, Inumaru walks through all the restaurants and public areas to check that things are running smoothly. Since the hotel attracts a high-profile clientele, part of each day is spent welcoming guests at the front door and escorting them to their rooms—a very important part of the hotelier's job. The rest of his day is spent at meetings. And then there are VIPs to be entertained in the evening.

Inumaru sees the hotel industry following current trends toward market specialization, with advanced technologies streamlining and enriching guest services: The Imperial has installed fax lines in each room as well as speaker phones. He explains that rooms are likely to become somewhat larger to accommodate sophisticated computer-related work spaces. The upper end of the market (the Imperial's clientele) will become more and more demanding as middle-range hotels offer improved facilities that were once the hallmarks of five-star hotels.

Citing "the personalized service factor" as crucial for luxury hotels, Inumaru says, "The market's deciding factor is likely to rest on which property has the more attractive ambiance, the stronger character, the better sense of taste . . ." And then he smiles as he adds, "To run a hotel, you must have great bathrooms."

And, from the look of things at the Imperial, you must have great shopping as well.

The arcade on the lower level is as much a part of the hotel's history as anything else. It dates back to 1922 and an idea that Tetsuzo Inumaru had to make things easier for Westerners in Tokyo who might otherwise be discouraged from going shopping because of rickshaw travel and the inevitable language barrier. He decided to import the arcade concept.

Inumaru made certain that merchants with branches outside the hotel maintained the same prices at both shops. His concerns were that the quality of the goods for sale and the prices charged would affect the way in which guests remembered the Imperial. The fifty arcade shops, all with English-speaking staff, run the gamut from couture to cough syrup, rare Japanese woodblock prints to Godiva chocolates, museum-quality Imari porcelain to Sony sound systems—and have become an attraction for the Japanese themselves.

One shop that attracts at least as many Tokyoites as guests is the Imperial's lobby-level gourmet extravaganza, Gargantua. It is strategically located across the street from the always-SRO Takarazuka Theater (a lavish all-female musical troupe) and across the corridor from the Imperial's equally popular Cycles Coffee Shop, which has become part of the Ginza-area itinerary for shoppers and businessmen alike. Gargantua, its name meant to imply bounty, is

where one can buy bread and cakes from the Imperial's bakery, and delicacies that include many internationally known brands as well as the Imperial's own line of frozen and canned specialities. There's a counter at which crowds vie for everything from foie gras and saumon fumé to bratwurst and Black Forest ham. Gifts of gourmet food being very popular in Japan, things get particularly busy after a wedding when out-of-town family members stop in for a tin of Gargantua coffee or tea, carrying their shopping bags home like merit badges.

The Imperial Tower opened in 1983, a 31-story annex designed to bring the hotel into the twenty-first century. Management added 353 deluxe guest rooms—the most spacious in Tokyo, with wide bay windows, huge bathtubs, and gold fixtures—to make a total of 1,120 for the hotel. The Tower has four shopping floors, fourteen floors of office space, and thirteen floors of guest rooms that peak with a recreational facility that includes massage rooms, saunas, showers, lounges, and a 17-meter pool with a glorious view of Tokyo Bay.

Gargantua—a gourmet paradise.

The pool.

Inauguration of the new president of Nissho Iwai trading company, held in the hotel's renovated Peacock Room (Kujaku-no-ma), and attended by 2,000 people. July 1990.

Designed to complement the Main Building, the Tower's exterior is of ceramic tile and semi-reflecting glass. Having offset the thirty-billion-yen construction cost via rental of some of the priciest commercial space in the world, the Imperial was able to maintain its standards of luxury. Its enviable 90-percent-plus occupancy rate is the highest in Tokyo.

One of the most arresting features of the Tower is the Imperial Plaza collection of designer boutiques spread over four floors of super-glitz. It is as though all the finest shops on the Champs-Elysées, the via Veneto, and Madison Avenue were relocated in one convenient location. This unique concept—there is no comparable concentration of chic anywhere else in the world—allows one to make the rounds at Chanel, Givenchy, Fendi, and Ferragamo

without facing the crowds on the Ginza. In the flash of a credit card, frogs are turned into princes and Cinderellas may gleefully retire their fairy godmothers.

To keep up one's strength, the Imperial has opened a Salon de Thé, where shoppers can refuel with pastries and cakes almost as rich as the shops. Surprisingly, there are almost as many men here as women. Because office space is so tight in Tokyo and privacy is at a premium, the "power" coffee break has become part of the daily business plan.

No sooner had the Tower opened than the main building was given a $71 million renovation. Then another $23 million was spent redesigning the hotel's largest banquet facility, the Peacock Room. Included in the ultra-modern design were motifs from Frank Lloyd Wright's original room:

The original Peacock Room, designed by Frank Lloyd Wright.

terracotta grillwork, brick and oya stone, and even turtleback-shaped chairs. Behind the scenes, the hotel installed the latest state-of-the-art electronics that control lighting, communications, environmental control, security, and audiovisual facilities.

Ichiro Inumaru has his eye on the day after tomorrow. Inumaru knows he must reinforce the infrastructure of the hotel as it begins its second century. Again setting a precedent for the Japanese hotel industry, the Imperial has introduced a five-day work week. Substantial time and funds are devoted to providing complete welfare systems for employees—growth is not measured merely in new buildings or renovations. The Imperial—whose success once depended on lessons from abroad—has learned that its greatest resource is itself.

The Imperial's status as Japan's premier hotel was most dramatically illustrated at the time of Emperor Hirohito's death in January 1989. The Imperial's own sense of history, and the role it has always played as its nation's unofficial host, was reflected in being first choice for those attending the funeral. Dignitaries from thirty-three countries booked into the hotel. Inumaru, an experienced statesman himself, assigned a single staff member as liaison to each embassy to ensure that individual requirements would be met.

Due to tight security precautions during this period, the hotel had to decline hundreds of private reservations. This, despite the fact that some floors remained largely vacant with the exception of a few rooms for dignitaries and security personnel. The degree to which the hotel staff became part of national protocol was demonstrated after the hotel was informed that the guests were to be received at the funeral at thirty-second intervals. The hotel's staff timed how many seconds it took to walk from each room to the elevator, from the elevator to the official limousines, and then the driving time to the location at which services were to be held. A complex schedule was worked out to avoid waiting time for elevators or at the receiving line.

The melancholy surrounding the formal period of mourning seemed somehow appropriate to the closing days of the hotel's first century. Japan was putting to rest more than its Emperor. The passing of Hirohito ended an era that had brought unparalleled devastation as well as a brilliant recovery that few would have dared predict. The nation no longer had the Showa emperor as a living reminder of its past. Japan was free to focus on its future as symbolized by the coronation of Crown Prince Akihito as the Heisei emperor.

But some things had not changed in a hundred years. Whether ending an era or beginning a new one, the Imperial Palace, in extending its hospitality to Japan's most important guests, was still dependent upon the Imperial Hotel.

Imperial Service

he Imperial Hotel is as demanding of employees as it is responsive to guests. While it would take a team of sociologists years to chart the long-term effects of Japanese management techniques on labor, its impact on guests is immediate. It works.

The reasons it works constitute a veritable catalog of revelations and contradictions, much like the Japanese themselves. The Imperial could not have existed, much less flourished, outside Japan. It sits not only in the center of Tokyo but at the heart of an enigma that has confounded everyone from Harvard MBAs to Silicon Valley CEOs.

Consider the following:

Firstly, a thirty-year-old assistant manager who has been at the hotel for six years is paid the same salary as a thirty-year-old bellman who has been at the hotel for six years. And they both receive the same annual bonus equal to 5.5 months' salary (2.5 months, paid on June 15 and 3 months on December 16). Less than one month's additional salary may be given in appreciation for excellence. Until an employee becomes a manager or the head of a department, the only factors for determining income are age and seniority.

Secondly, there is no tipping in Japan. Instead, a 10-percent service charge is added to the bill in restaurants and hotels. Taxi drivers do not expect to be tipped. Porters have fees. Unlike "no tipping" in Western hotels, the Imperial means it. Tips will be handed back with a polite no-thank-you. In a society where company loyalty has a higher priority than ego or personal gain, it is not dignified to serve two masters. And this is not a country in which dignity is an optional extra: it is instinctive.

The Imperial was the first hotel in Japan to add a 10-percent service charge. Guests complained initially because they were accustomed to tipping only for good service. But in the postwar 1950s, Japan had not yet performed any economic miracles and had no standing as a creditor nation—it was a place for sightseeing, subject to the ups and downs of seasonal travel. Tourists came in spring to see the cherry blossoms, and then again in the autumn. But few came in winter or summer, and hotel workers had long stretches during which they were unable to supplement their low wages with tips.

The only way to guarantee workers a steady annual income was to raise pay and initiate a service charge that would, over the course of a year, reimburse the hotel for having "advanced" money to the staff. The benefit of such a system, to the hotel, is worker flexibility. A waiter in the Imperial's showcase restaurant, Fontainebleau, can be transferred to the coffee shop without fear that his income will be reduced. It is expected that his ego will remain intact because his income remains intact. Also, he has the satisfaction of pitching in when the company needs him. Conversely, a bellman with special aptitude can be transferred to a more important job without any immediate increase in salary.

Such is the "open-floor" principle on which Japanese business operates: there are no private offices except on the very highest level. For most workers, there is no geographic hierarchy. People who work for the company, in no matter what department, work together. Literally.

The Imperial hires some 120 people per year—but only after each has had as many as ten interviews with different department heads, all the way up to the managing director. Primarily concerned with the applicants' humanity, ability to work hard, and personality, interviewers focus on understanding personal philosophies: they know they're selecting the next generation of managers. While Western individualists fear fractured egos as the price for joining a company team, there is no denying the satisfaction of being approved by that entire team and entering a perk-laden lifetime employment system.

The Imperial grades employees three times a year. Those with low ratings are spoken to and perhaps transferred to another department. However, all employees are asked annually whether they wish to change jobs within the company. Since outsiders are rarely brought in above entry-level positions, there is a tangible chain of succession. At age 60, employees retire with a cash bonus equal to 55 months' pay. While salaries are generally lower than in the U.S., the trade-off is job security.

Each year, nearly one hundred of the Imperial's roomboys check into the hotel for a night. Bellmen escort them to their rooms as though they were regular guests. They spend the night, watch TV, take showers, and order breakfast from room service. Half as many Imperial housekeepers and higher-level personnel are taken to another city, perhaps Hong Kong, to check into a posh hotel and meet with their counterparts in order to exchange information.

Kiyohito Minoshima, after attending Cornell's School of Hotel Administration in the 1960s, began at the Imperial as a $30 per month roomboy. He was a waiter for six months, then worked in the front office and later became manager of the theater restaurant in the Imperial. In the sixties, he was sent on the road with the unenviable task of having to convince the same generation of Americans who had fought the Japanese that Tokyo was now an ideal place for a vacation or conference.

Minoshima, who is today a managing director of the Imperial, knew that once he

Toshiko Takeya in a VIP suite.

had been hired by the hotel his future would be limited only by his capabilities. (It is difficult to imagine an American college graduate accepting a roomboy entry-level position.) He credits much of what we view as management success directly to the quality of a Japanese labor market that is well educated and not afraid to start at the bottom.

Before I begin, I stand in front of the mirror, because a mirror reflects the spirit of a person. If I am troubled in mind—something a guest can sense—the mirror will tell me so.

Toshiko Takeya is 82 years old and has been working at the Imperial since she was 25. Among the first group of women to be hired by the hotel, Takeya-san had nine brothers, a sick mother, and a father whose business was failing.

It was 1933 and she considered herself fortunate to get the job, even though the workday for room maids was from seven to seven, with only one day off a month. Twice a week, she had to stay over in the hotel for night service. Her starting salary was nine yen a month. Some 57 years later, she still comes to work daily, but now she supervises the room attendants on the Imperial's VIP floor. A senior ambassador of charm and manners, her status as a near national treasure has been assured by her having received a citation for service from the emperor.

In contrast, one of Takeya-san's newest recruits has a workday that runs from 8:00 A.M.—4:15 P.M. and receives a starting salary of 172,000 yen a month with eight days off each month. Watching these women as they sit side by side, one is touched by the sincerity of the mutual regard they have for each other. Yet, at least to Western eyes, could they be more different? One is tall, straight-backed, head up; the other, graceful as a willow, leans forward slightly, head tilted to signal she is listening only to you, hair long and lustrous but tied back softly. Nine yen a month versus 172,000 yen a month. In 1933, 10 kilos of white rice cost almost two yen—in 1990 the figure is about ¥4,000. In 1933 a double room at the Imperial Hotel cost 15 yen a night—in 1990 it is ¥30,000. The figures will not let go. Nor will the presumption that these two women could not possibly have anything in common. Americans, having grown up in a country whose greatest achievement was to reject the previous generation's lifestyle, have only to witness the bond between these women to sense what being Japanese means.

The young woman explains that she admires Takeya-san most because she is right every time. She has the experience to know precisely the correct thing to do in order to make a guest feel comfortable. And to never show that she is tired or perhaps not feeling well. Takeya-san, on the other hand, has the generosity to recognize the pressures on new staff members who are dependent upon so many other people.

In the 1930s, Takeya-san recalls, her work day began by serving guests breakfast in bed. She would go to each room with a menu, take the order, go to the kitchen, get the food, and carry it back. She smiles, recalling a guest who ordered soft-boiled eggs. Takeya-san thought it would be helpful to peel the eggs and put them into another dish. She even cut the eggs open for him. Day after day, he would order eggs. Day after day, she would peel and cut them open. But he never ate the eggs. Finally, she asked about it: He hadn't eaten them because her extra service had made them cold.

It was the adjustment to Western customs and the English language, far more than the physical rigors of the job, that proved most difficult for her in the beginning. Takeya-san's biggest problem was not learning how to make a bed or sweep a floor, but rather to learn the English words for bed and floor. In those days, less than 5 percent of the clientele were Japanese. Had Takeya-san been hired today, she would have had to pass up to ten interviews, one conducted in English. Instead of adjusting to Western customs, her main challenge would have been learning to coordinate her job with the room service waiter, the valet, the porter, etc. Today, she checks the list of guests to ensure that she addresses them properly and by name. But when she was first hired, it was considered improper for the staff to call guests by name: "Sir" or "Madam" were the only acceptable greetings.

In those days, once the guest left the room, she would begin to clean, make the beds, take the linens to the laundry, and be ready to serve lunch in the room. In the late afternoon, she cleaned the rugs by sprinkling Japanese tea leaves and shreds of wet newspaper onto them and then sweeping them up. Later, guests ordered drinks, which she would bring to their rooms. It was a time in which men wore tuxedos and women wore gowns. She would catch a hint of perfume in the corridor as they left for dinner and she knew from the scent which of her guests had gone. Then it was time for evening service and, on the nights she stayed over in the hotel, she would polish their shoes after they went to sleep.

A smile comes to her face. Takeya-san always liked the old Frank Lloyd Wright building. The lighting was soft, indirect. She would stand on the third-floor rooftop and look down, feeling as though she were in a castle. But she often wound up playing Cinderella: The building's facade was as fragile as her dream. There were leaks and she often had to use a mop and pail to keep up with them.

Takeya-san has long since put away her mop and pail. There is nothing fragile about the new Imperial. It conveys a sense of luxury that is neither pretentious nor trendy. No matter the endless social and business hubbub of the public rooms, the Imperial has never forgotten that "a hotel sells tranquillity and quiet." This concept has been translated into calm colors, rich textures, deep carpets, and solid wooden furniture. Rooms that are already large by traditional Japanese standards appear even bigger because of the expansive windows that overlook Hibiya Park and the palace grounds. Bathrooms are white marble with a wall-to-wall mirror that has a "no-fog" area over the vanity. Amenities are replenished daily along with lots of thick fresh towels. One has the feeling of staying with an old-monied relative whose aim is to make you feel comfortable, not impress you with his wealth.

The Imperial Suite, the largest facility in any hotel in Japan for hosting official guests, covers 508 square meters, and has bullet-proof doors and access to the roof for a quick escape by helicopter, if

The elegance of the Imperial Suite; the wall panel is in the manner of a Japanese screen painting.

necessary. There's a baby grand piano in the sumptuous living room, and a full dining room and kitchen in addition to numerous bedrooms and baths. All furniture and fabrics are specially made with an eye to appearing regal and stately rather than glamorous. Accordingly, the price per night is a princely $4,000.

A week prior to a VIP's arrival, Takeya-san's staff receives a photograph of the guest, his or her spouse if they are coming, and a briefing on the country's customs and cuisine. The kitchen staff has also been alerted to religious or cultural preferences which may include food prepared at the guest's embassy or even a personal chef in attendance. At times, the suite must be readied with burning incense and special prayer rugs. All in a day's work.

When the Imperial Hotel first opened, the emperor's master of court ceremonies taught the staff how to wait upon all guests as they did at the palace. For example, if a staff member saw a guest in the hallway, the staff member would move to the left, stop, bow, and wait for the guest to pass. Only after the guest had gone by would the staff member resume walking. Takeya-san remembers that since she had to wait for the guest to pass with her head bowed, she rarely had a chance to see what they looked like—despite being so close. Today, such treatment is reserved for official visitors. The Imperial makes an exception for those who were once VIPs. "We always provide them with the same service as before."

Takeya-san, who once carried blocks of ice on her back from the kitchen to the upstairs pantries, agrees that service today is much more efficient, but old habits are hard to break. To this day, when Takeya-san goes to sleep, she never puts her feet in the direction of the hotel—a sign of respect.

The Imperial has 1,671 employees, not including banquet waiters and part-timers. It has 410 cooks who make 20,000 meals a day. The third biggest user of water in Tokyo, the hotel's monthly water bill is over $370,000. Electricity tops the utilities expense at nearly $700,000 per month, with telephones a mere $255,000-plus. The main building has 712 rooms; the Tower building has 353.

The Imperial Hotel has its own union. A common practice in Japan, a company-wide union makes it possible for the hotel to customize benefits that match the needs of its own employees—and it puts pressure on the Imperial to keep salaries in step with the high standards it demands. Most of all, in a system that features lifetime employment, it strengthens the mutual dependence between management and staff, a bond that exhibits itself in more informal ways: the Imperial is the only hotel to have

its own rugby team. They play the workers from the Tsukiji Fish Market. Since no member of the staff with bruises would ever be allowed to greet guests, waiters and front-desk personnel cannot play unless scheduled for a couple of days off after the game. A literal example of "saving face."

It is often said that the most important person at a hotel is the doorman. He is the first staff member to be seen by guests, and the last. His behavior greatly affects their feelings about the hotel. An inappropriate welcome is the most difficult of slights from which to recoup. Fortunately, this is a view also held by Nobuo Tomita, who has been the Imperial's doorman for over twenty years. "I can recognize about 1,500 regular guests by name—I always read the papers, especially the economic news, and memorize the names and faces of prominent businessmen who might use the Imperial." Tomita, who wears out shoes faster than Baryshnikov, takes a short break every few hours—"to rest my feet and study the guest list."

The doorman, Nobuo Tomita, with the hotel's limousine.

Front reception is considered the most difficult position in a hotel. It's the first place everyone heads with a problem, but the last place anyone goes when things run smoothly. Says one member of the front office, "We are the hotel's 'software'." People checking in are tired and cranky from a long trip, and those checking out are always in a hurry. This is where someone complains because he has a room on 15 (and a fear of heights) but didn't request a low floor earlier, or because he arrived without a reservation and there are no rooms available. No one ever stops by to say, "Hi, I'm having a great time!"

The five people on duty must act as psychiatrists, magicians, and best friends. For yet another example of "saving face," wait for the limousine bus to arrive from dreaded Narita Airport (too far, too crowded). There's sure to be someone with lots of Teutonic, Anglo, or Stateside impatience ready to burst into flame. After all, it works back home. "Don't tell *me* you're fully booked!"

Welcome to Japan. With the dignity of Mt. Fuji and as impervious to threatening weather, the front desk responds not in kind, but kindly. Not only is there no such thing as confrontation in this country, but all available adrenaline is routed toward helping the guest maintain his dignity—and finding him a room somewhere else.

The reservations office is directly behind the front desk. Eight people with eight phones sit at eight chairs around an octagonal table facing a wall-sized chart of room prices and dates. A red dot indicates that rooms at that price have been reserved for that date. Reservations clerks note requests from compulsive gamblers who want to have "lucky" room numbers as well as special security arrangements required for diplomats and celebrities. Duly noted, all files are fed into computers that produce daily lists for the front desk to use in assigning rooms and registering guests.

It is this updated roster of who is "in" and who is "out" that allows the head housekeeper to schedule which rooms are to be made up first—and how. Japanese guests are more likely to use the robe and slippers provided by the hotel and they must be on prominent display. Also, if a guest is Japanese and only one bed is being used, the bed near the wall is made up. However, if the guest is American, the bed near the window is made up. The day list also tells the housekeeper which language newspaper is to be delivered at 6:00 A.M. when the breakfast crew arrives.

That same list is also integral to the smooth running of the hotel's computerized switchboard. Housed in a setting that more closely resembles an operating room than a hotel, the switchboard consoles are in a soundproof, glassed-in, air-conditioned space on a raised, carpeted floor that hides all the cables and phone wires. Shoes off, slippers on, if you wish to enter. "Our voice reflects our state of mind," says Setsuko Inoue, who oversees a staff trained to handle some 9,000 calls per day. She believes in creating an environment that fosters calm and tranquillity.

Women operators sit at rows of computer terminals for 90-minute shifts. Because of the stress of the job, Imperial operators work only a total of four hours a day (three shifts with 30-minute breaks in between). No man has ever answered the phone at the Imperial because, according to Inoue, "a woman's voice is more pleasant over the phone."

The wall in front of the operators has a world time chart, a clock, a calendar, names of VIPs currently at the hotel, departmental managers, whom to contact in the event of an emergency, world maps, restaurant hours—a daily changing mural of hotel hieroglyphics.

Morning wakeup calls (in five languages) are computerized during peak periods. However, for the operators at the switchboard, 9:00 A.M. to 11:30 A.M. is the busiest time. When a guest calls the operator, his name and room number flash on a screen. He is greeted by name and in the proper language. Imperial operators are trained to answer on the third ring—anything sooner would startle the guest.

What is startling, and pleasantly so, are the greetings one receives all during the course of a day. A bellman, walking down the corridor wheeling a cart filled with luggage, pauses to bow, saying, "Good afternoon, sir." A maid, on her way to bringing fresh towels, stops to enquire, "How are you today, sir?" There is virtually no way to pass a member of the staff without being greeted. And there is virtually no way to misinterpret the greeting—it is a well-spoken, not gratuitously muttered, eyeball-to-eyeball acknowledgment of your presence, an extraordinary display of hospitality. It is impossible to be a non-person at the Imperial.

Even when calling to have your laundry collected, a display lights up with your name and the operator greets you personally. Tell her that you have a food stain on your jacket and she'll enquire where you ate last night. Les Saisons? Fontainebleau? The Rainbow Room? The plot thickens as she then asks what you ate. No, she's not playing Hercule Poirot. The kitchens at the Imperial give the laundry a copy of the recipe for each dish served so that when a guest has a stain, they know exactly what caused it and how to make it disappear. Each time new dishes are added to the menus, a copy of the recipe is given to the laundry.

As though that weren't enough, the laundry has "magic" button boxes, fed through the years by laundry magpies until they have become a virtual encyclopedia of buttons. Lost one? Chances are, you find a close enough match to fool everyone until you get back home.

A team of young women at the elevators in the lobby greet and guide all guests. "Good evening," one says as you wait for the elevator doors to open. You step inside, notice a fresh rose in the bud vase, and face front. Then, just as the doors begin to close, in a tricky bit of choreography, she bows low and says, "Thank you for waiting," when there was barely any wait at all.

It has an effect. As other guests get on, even those with urban chips on their shoulders greet one another like club members who wouldn't think of passing by without a friendly word. For one brief shining elevator ride, there is a hint of Camelot.

Backstage at the hotel—the message service.

Imperial Weddings

**S**etting the date for a wedding is a very serious matter. Beyond an obvious preference for Sundays and holidays in the spring and fall, there is the search for a "lucky" day. The Japanese lunar calendar uses a six-day cycle to identify unlucky days, semi-lucky ones, and those propitious days known as *taian* on which most people want to hold the ceremony. They believe, or at least hope, that choosing a lucky day assures the future success and prosperity of the marriage. Predictably, there are only a few *taian* Sundays each year, and they are premium dates to reserve.

On any of them, the Imperial may host as many as twenty-two weddings which translates into serving 3,400 people an eight- or nine-course lunch or dinner. Small wonder that nuptials account for some 20 percent of the hotel's income and for an even larger percentage of its reputation.

The Imperial, firmly established throughout Japan as *the* "event" hotel, caters for over one thousand wedding banquets a year. Almost any weekend one can step into the main lobby and become an instant member of the wedding. No one will ask who you are. Certainly not the platoon of tuxedoed young men who've never worn anything more formal than a school blazer and are huddling together for social security. Nor will any of the nervous young women who are pretending they actually know how to sit down in a traditional costume that has a mind of its own. Kimono-clad in-laws bow as they meet for the first time, a blushing bride is hurried through the lobby by her pale and breathless mother, while cousins who haven't seen one another since the last wedding trade jokes as intently as stock tips. Friday night, and all day Saturday and Sunday, there is a nearly seamless procession of wedding parties marching to a drummer that has lasted longer than any of the marriages: the Imperial itself.

The Japanese, having redefined conspicuous consumption as a rigorous diet of name brands, from designer chocolates to Rockefeller Center, are no less attentive to corporate logos when selecting the venue for a wedding. Thus, in a nation where children characterize their fathers' careers by employer (my father works for Sony, Mitsubishi, or Toshiba) rather than by profession (my father is an engineer, salesman, or lawyer), it is not surprising that young couples who are determined to launch their married lives with a top-of-the-line salvo are willing to wait a year for an available slot in the Imperial's schedule.

As Japan modernized, so did the concept of where to have the wedding—from homes to shrines to hotels. Especially in a crowded city like Tokyo, most families do not have homes large enough to accommodate events like weddings. It was especially innovative of hotelier Tetsuzo Inumaru in the 1920s to bring the shrine into the hotel and arrange for a local Shinto priest to officiate. Ironically, the hotel that had been established to convince its foreign guests that Japan was in step with the West has become an integral part of Japanese culture. The reflection of the West that the Imperial Hotel hoped to mirror is, today, precisely the image that the Japanese have of themselves.

Weddings are still the most important rite of passage in Japanese life. As formalized an event as ever, only the surrounding circumstances have changed. No longer are all marriages arranged, and most newlyweds have adopted the Western custom of going on a honeymoon. Weddings in Japan are lavish. Traditionally, they were paid for by the groom's father, who decided where the event would take place and how many people would be invited. Not any longer. At least, not in Tokyo, where the bride makes the final decision on where to hold the wedding—as well as whom to marry. This is a far cry from the arranged marriage of the past in which everything from spouse to hors d'œuvres was decided upon by parents or feudal lords.

The price for this new independence is that the bride and groom usually wind up paying half the cost, with each of their families contributing the balance. This mutual investment between new in-laws serves to strengthen ties: The more extravagant and expensive the wedding, the more it signifies the unity and approval of the families involved.

There is a calm, quiet area on the mezzanine at the Imperial where brides-to-be and their mothers meet with the hotel's wedding consultants to map out a strategy. The consultant's desk is piled high with banquet menus, charts for seating arrangements, photos of floral displays, as well as elaborate brochures showing all variations on the theme in different price categories. The brides-to-be pore over the information as though decoding the Rosetta Stone. There are whispered conferences between mother and daughter, calming words of encouragement from the consultant.

Every now and then a chef can be seen joining the discussion to explain that a foie gras mousse can indeed be substituted for the smoked salmon soufflé. Decisions on whether to go with filet for the main course rather than prime ribs of beef, how many tiers for the cake, and whether to serve a Bordeaux or a Burgundy take place

This room at the second Imperial Hotel was converted to a Shinto ceremonial hall when necessary.

Wedding reception at the first Imperial Hotel, 1920. (Courtesy of Mrs. Matsu Fukuma)

Wedding reception in the Peacock Room of the second Imperial Hotel, 1925.

A thoroughly modern marriage, 1927. (Courtesy of *Sekai Gaho*)

while attendants serve traditional green tea. No matter which choices are made, the wedding will be precisely what the bride dreamed it would be. After all, this is the Imperial.

The cost per guest for an Imperial wedding is some $300—including flowers and pictures, but not including the customary gift for each guest or rental of the bride's wedding kimono, which can amount to as much as one million yen before anyone would think about raising an eyebrow. With the average wedding party checking in at 130–140 people, the tab hovers at around $40,000. On the credit side, guests arriving for a wedding banquet stop at the reception table to pick up their seating arrangements and to drop off their white

Wedding reception in the present hotel's Fuji Room (Fuji-no-ma), June 17, 1990. The groom's witness is standing next to him and next to the bride is the witness's wife.

envelopes. Ceremonies held at the Imperial usually net the happy couple something between $200–300 per envelope—unless, of course, you happen to have a favorite uncle or a very wealthy cousin willing to underwrite an even larger portion of the festivities.

The Big Day generally begins the night before, with the arrival of the bride and her mother. And their cosmetics and gowns: The wedding is an event at which the bride is required to change costumes four times. By 8:30 A.M., the bride is putting on her makeup, having her hair done, and starting to deal with the mysteries of a kimono. Between 10:00 and 11:00, she sees members of her family, including the groom. But the most important visitor is her father. Alone with him in her dressing room, she thanks him for taking care of her.

The banquet floors at the hotel are lined with rooms where families meet for a quick toast before the ceremony. Since there can be as many as ten weddings going on at the same time, the Imperial's staff must time things with the precision of a missile launching. Couples go from dressing room to ceremonial room to photographer to dressing room to reception line to banquet room to dressing room to banquet room with nary a mid-marital collision.

By 11:00, the immediate family has gathered for the Shinto ceremony. They are dressed either in dark, formal kimonos or quite somber modern clothes. The bride wears an all-white kimono and traditional matching hood. The groom wears a black kimono with long culottes known as *hakama*. The two families sit facing one another at long tables lining opposite sides of a fragrant cypress-and-cedar-paneled room.

The ceremonial hall, with the bride's family on the left and the groom's on the right. The ceremony is about to begin. June 29, 1990.

A Shinto priest officiates in the center. The ceremony unites not only the couple being married but their families as well. All the bonds are sealed by drinking sake.

Within half an hour, the families have relocated to the photo studio, where a rather solemn group picture is taken. The bride and groom stay on for more animated shots while the families go into the foyer to greet guests.

By 12:30 the bride has changed into her million-yen kimono and joins the reception line to greet guests. An interesting wrinkle on the "best man/maid of honor" custom is that the groom selects instead a "witness," essentially a political appointee, since he's usually someone in a position of authority where the groom works. The witness's wife assumes the role accorded maid of honor in the West.

After cocktails have been served, the guests are seated in the banquet room where a master of ceremonies takes over. The MC is sometimes a well-known television personality, hired for the afternoon to lend brand-name credibility to the proceedings. As the couple enters, a band plays a well-known tune they have selected—it may be anything from the wedding march to the theme from *Ghostbusters*. Everyone applauds as the couple walks to the dais and bows to their guests. At the groom's place the napkin is folded like a crane, the bride's is folded like a turtle—both are symbols of longevity.

Then comes the hard part: up to an hour of speeches, during which no food or beverages are served. First, the witness officially announces to the room that the wedding has taken place. He proceeds to embark on a 20-minute history of the family. Then the groom's most honored guest

The priest offers the bride a toast of sake.

makes a speech, followed by the bride's most honored guest's speech. At this point, the young couple ceremoniously cuts the cake and a toast is offered, an event that occasions dinner and a series of speeches lasting anywhere from one to ten minutes each.

Upon sighting the hors d'œuvres, the bride leaves and slips into either a Western-style wedding gown, complete with veil and train, or another kimono (her third change). The groom switches from traditional garb into a tuxedo. Before you can say *filet de bœuf*, the happy couple reenters the banquet hall in modern dress. This once symbolic changing of clothes (*oiro-naoshi*—the transition from white to colored kimono signified the transition from innocence to adulthood). Today it has become more a fashion statement than a cultural one but is no less integral a part of the celebration.

A few bites of food and the bride is off to replace her wedding gown with an evening dress. She's back before dessert arrives. Interestingly, wedding cake isn't eaten at the wedding. Slices are put into boxes and given to guests to take home in a shopping bag along with the couple's thank-you gift—the current trend is toward top-quality silverware. You can always tell a departing wedding party in the lobby by their telltale Imperial Hotel shopping bags.

By 4:00 P.M., after lots of food and music (there is no dancing at a Japanese wedding), the MC brings the banquet to a close. Guests make their way to the reception line to wish the young couple well. After every out-of-town uncle has been thanked for coming, the bride changes for the last time into a disco dress to wear at a second party with a group of friends.

At last, it is time to dance.

Group photograph of bride and groom with the family members who attended the Shinto ceremony.

Imperial Kitchens

A t 7:30 each morning, a young cook turns on the main steam switch that heats caldrons large enough to parboil a person. By 8:00 A.M., the rest of the brigade arrives. They wear white shirts and aprons, striped work trousers, tall white toques, and white rubber boots because the floor is about to get slippery and wet.

Making soup stock is an entry-level job. Younger generation cooks are allowed to start the consommé on the theory that the beginning is not as important as the finish. First, the cooks slice carrots and onions. Then they wash bones saved from the previous day's butchering. (Stocks are made daily, whether in short supply or not, because the ingredients are perishable.) Vegetables and bones are portioned by eye into large containers. Ladles of egg whites are added. The young cooks kneel before the pans, like novitiates in some bizarre culinary order. But instead of praying, they reach into the pans and blend in the egg whites.

By now a dozen men are hard at work, each creating his own sound effects: the *tap*, *tap*, *tap* of rapid slicing, the hollow splash of water falling into the steam-heated caldrons, the thuds as heavy buckets filled with bones are slammed down, the clanging of pots, the scrape of metal on metal, the squeak of rubber boots on the tile floor.

Bones and vegetables are poured into the steaming caldrons. Seasonings are stirred in with wooden spoons large enough to propel a small canoe. The men work with precision despite the steam and the noise, and, most of all, despite the heat. Egg whites rise to the top, clarifying the stock by carrying aloft all the behind-the-scenes flotsam and jetsam. The cooks skim off the

untidy residue again and again to create the crystal-clear consommé that is the mother's milk of French cuisine—the rich stocks that nourish soups and sauces.

The stock that begins at eight in the morning will be ready by two or three in the afternoon, but not before it has passed Chef Mori, "The Saltmaster." He is the Imperial's soup chef, the only man in the supply center kitchen allowed to add salt to the stock. With years of experience and a palate that holds a degree in perfection, one imagines him taking a sip of the day's broth and smiling as he says, "Ah, yes. Tuesday!"

Two consommés are made: Coffee House Consommé in which chicken bouillon is used, and a purist version for restaurants and banquets. Special stocks, such as those prepared for the hotel's classic French dining room, Fontainebleau, fea-

Chef Mori manning the stock pots.

ture mineral water as a key ingredient. However, the restaurants usually make their own specialty stocks—duck, veal, etc.

The heart of the food service operation at the Imperial is the supply center in a sub-basement two levels below the street. It is here that fruits and vegetables are delivered daily, fresh bread is baked, and meat is inspected and butchered. The Imperial's kitchen steward is the man responsible for ordering and receiving all the supplies needed by all the chefs in all the kitchens. After twenty-four years on the front line as a maitre d', he knows firsthand the quality of food required for cooking and presentation.

Each restaurant anticipates its needs by two to three days and sends order slips to the steward, who then tallies them onto a computerized master shopping list. Simple. But what about the thirty-five extra orders each day for special items or sudden culinary inspirations? In addition, he's likely to receive 300 bills daily from suppliers. And don't forget that he's got to keep track of who ordered what and be certain it arrives on time. Not to mention storing everything properly. The supply center must have enough staples on hand for five restaurants, two coffee shops, a traditional Japanese teahouse, two bars that serve snacks, room service for 1,100 rooms, and banquet halls that serve an army of people. Plus an employee cafeteria.

Most important, the steward is responsible for seeing that every single item received is right. But "right" doesn't simply mean receiving melons if he ordered melons, or getting the right number of melons, or even the right type of melons: it means the *best* melons. And that doesn't simply mean the best tasting ones either. As with produce, everything must be uniform in size for the recipes to work. Each melon must be bigger than one kilogram.

For banquets, they are cut into six pieces; for restaurants, only five. In Tokyo, where melons can retail for between $30 and $90 *each*, when the Imperial buys melons, the

A perfect—and expensive—melon.

SOME ITEMS FROM THE HOTEL'S
ANNUAL SHOPPING LIST

From Australia:
  Lobster tails / 2024 kg
  Whole lobsters / 2300 kg
  Processed lobster / 30,450 350-gram
            packages
  Shrimp / 1625 kg
  Abalone / 4949 cans
  Lamb / 9288 kg
  Asparagus / 126,121 stalks
  Endives / 513 cartons

From West Germany:
  Wine—19,325 bottles at a cost
      of $125,000

From Norway:
  Smoked salmon / 6014 kg
  Atlantic fresh salmon / 9041 kg
  Herring packed in wine / 2282 kg

From France:
  Wine—142,000 bottles at a cost
      of $2,400,000

From Denmark:
  Cheese at a cost of $7500

From the USA:
  Beef and Veal / $2,880,000
  Oranges and grapefruits / $4,176,000

market feels the effect. All citrus fruit is imported, some 700 cases of oranges per month from California. Tomatoes grown domestically for La Brasserie come 28 to a box, but for the premier restaurant, Fontainebleau, they must be larger—24 to a box.

Deliveries are received in a large open area adjacent to an underground ramp where trucks arrive each morning with precision: eggs and milk at 8:30 A.M., vegetables at 9:20, meat at 9:45, and fruit at 11:00.

As produce is delivered, cartons are opened to check for quality. Lining the corridor, the fruit and vegetable applicants are as varied as any truckload of raw recruits: large orange carrots straight from a farm in Hokkaido, elegant reed-slim scallions in chic designer wooden crates, long-stemmed cress covered in cellophane, packages of edible orchids for plate decora-

tions, cartons of skinless onions that have been hydrogen-blown to remove their skins, packets of fresh herbs—chervil, thyme, and mint wrapped as lovingly as wedding bouquets. By 10:00 A.M., all refrigerator space is filled. Perishables are held for only three days before being replaced automatically by fresh goods.

In-house deliveries are then made to the Imperial's restaurants. Because supply center staff are not dressed in proper kitchen whites, they are not permitted to handle high-ticket items such as fish and meat, which are picked up by restaurant staff.

The king of the high-ticket items is Chef Matsubara. Deceptively mild-mannered with his pleasant smile and eyeglasses, this 35-year veteran of the beef wars is primed for combat. Indeed, the moment he enters the cutting room, he becomes a veritable samurai, long knife unsheathed and at his side. He strides along a stainless steel

Produce being inspected after delivery.

Chef Matsubara conducting the meat examination.

counter strewn with tenderloins, sirloins, and the hopes of his supplier. Standing by are hotel staff ready to weigh the 3,800 pounds of meat delivered daily. Pacing in the background is one of the accountants from the supply department. Small wonder: the annual beef bill is more than two million dollars.

The room is dead silent except for an occasional grunt of disapproval as Matsubara raises his "sword" and in a single stroke slashes off that portion of excess fat for which he does not wish to be charged. Then he cuts away another layer of fat to see the color of the meat and feel its texture. The best beef will be firm to the touch. He shakes his head. The meat is too soft. Too red. It has not been aged properly. Another grunt. The butchers on the other side of the counter quickly take the offending loin away.

But not before the accountant locks eyes with the supplier as if to say, "One for our side." Matsubara continues along the counter, making the first cut for the assistant butchers, a line of demarcation to show them precisely where to remove the short ribs. In so doing, he has defined each roast to be certain it conforms to his high standards. (The loin that wasn't properly aged, but was still good quality, has been put aside for another day.) The rest of the meat is then placed on trays and identified with a tag that includes: name of supplier, type of cut, weight, and price. (Domestic Kobe beef is even more expensive than imported beef: Sirloin is ¥4,000/200 g.) Later, a dozen men will trim and slice to comply with the restaurant chefs' specifications. Over the course of a year, they will handle some 700 tons.

Weighing in at 550 kg of flour and 1000 liters of milk per day is the Imperial bakery, one of the country's first to bake bread. In 1911, when Baron Okura was still chairman of the hotel, he met Ivan Sagoyan, baker to the imperial court of the czar. After the revolution, Sagoyan (understandably unemployed) was invited to establish a bakery at the Imperial, thus beginning Japan's formal introduction to the Western bread products that have become part of Tokyo's daily food vocabulary. Half the output is used by the hotel, and half goes on sale in the hotel's gourmet shop, Gargantua.

The man currently in charge of the bakery is Katsumi Sugashima, who has spent 37 years developing a sense of smell far more reliable than any oven thermometer. A deep breath lets him know precisely when the bread is ready. Automatic timing devices cannot compensate for climatic changes that make the yeast respond differently. "Bread has a life of its own," he says.

The life it has at the Imperial begins at 3:30 A.M. with a few of the bakery's 32 workers who stayed at the hotel overnight to ensure fresh bread for the breakfast service. The first of the 35 types of bread to be made are breadsticks; the most popular bread is the ubiquitous baguette. Everything baked until the second shift closes down shop at 4:00 P.M. is delivered hot from the oven to the supply center. They are then routed to individual restaurants for use in dining rooms, banquet halls, and room service.

The first interaction of the day between kitchen and guest actually begins the night before with those maddening little breakfast cards that ask more questions than a tax auditor. They are collected from door knobs every time a bellman or waiter walks through the hallway. The room service order clerk then makes up a master sheet by time and floor.

The morning breakfast crew arrives at 6:00 A.M. to find the breakfast carts already lining the corridors outside the mezzanine room service kitchen. Waiters have been assigned floors and the first thing they do is arrange the carts chronologically as they set them with china, crystal, and silverware. Meanwhile, room service clerks are taking last-minute orders on the phone. High up in the Rainbow Room, the crew begins to assemble the breakfast buffet. Across the corridor, the staff at another of the hotel's restaurants, Les Saisons (their kitchen is the one used for room service), is busy setting tables.

By the time the bud vases are on the carts, the waiters have begun shouting, in Japanese, their orders to the cooks: "7:15 to 7:30, I need six eggs easy over, three with bacon, two crisp, one with sausage." Coffee and teapots have been readied, juice poured; butter, marmalade, fresh rolls, and ice water are all in place, awaiting the hot dishes. Experienced voyeurs can always tell which carts are destined for the Tower: lots of bran cereals for the movers and shakers who stay there.

Incredibly, the chefs flip French toast and make omelettes using chopsticks. It is a show of dexterity that deserves musical accompaniment. Unmoved by performance art, the 7:15 to 7:30 waiter takes his hot plates and, after a deep breath, pushes a trainload of carts into one of the special elevators used only for room service, disappearing as the doors close behind him.

On days that I cook, I eat lunch at eleven. Things often taste better than they really are when you're hungry—which is why you cook better after you have eaten.

Nobuo Murakami's parents died when he was a little boy. He had two uncles—one was a tailor and one was a carpenter. The question was: Whose business would he go

Trolleys lined up for the breakfast room service.

Making omelettes Imperial-style.

into? The young boy thought and thought. You buy a suit perhaps once every five years. You buy a house once in a lifetime. But you must eat every day. He would become a cook.

After interviewing for a job at the Imperial, his application was put at the bottom of the pile. He stopped by periodically. Slowly, very slowly, his name moved up the list. The young man's persistence and determination impressed the personnel manager. His application was placed closer to the top—which meant a wait of *only two years* before there might be an opening.

Murakami couldn't wait. He took jobs at various restaurants, gaining experience until his name reached the top of the pile at the Imperial. Finally, he had become what he most wanted to be—an employee of the Imperial Hotel. Some fifty years later, Nobuo Murakami is still what he most wants to be.

But he is also something he never dreamed of becoming: the most famous chef in Japan.

Since 1958, Chef Murakami has been the nation's leading authority on French cuisine. He has had a television program on NHK, Japan's national broadcasting network, is a widely published author of many cookbooks, and even has a line of gourmet food products with his picture on the label. He was the first Japanese chef to be accorded membership in the Chaines des Rotisseurs. Today, he is not only executive chef of the Imperial—the man to whom chefs Mori, Matsubara, Sugashima, and the more than 400 cooks who turn out 20,000 meals a day are responsible—but he is also the hotel's senior managing director.

When hiring a chef, Murakami looks first for health, then strong will. In most instances, he does not want someone who has worked elsewhere. Most of the chefs heading the Imperial's restaurants have been there for over 30 years—but they must still submit all changes in the menu for approval.

Despite his powerful build, one would never think that the bespectacled, modest man who is always quick to smile and is a master calligrapher, holds a black belt in judo. He says judo helps keep him calm in the kitchen. Dressed in his chef's whites, seated in his office amid walls lined with awards and smiling photos, Murakami is as personable as the cuisine he creates. Predictably, his face always lights up when he talks about food.

In 1940, when Murakami began to work at the Imperial, Bunjiro Ishiwatari was head chef, and the American-style kitchen that Tetsuzo Inumaru had designed for Frank Lloyd Wright was the finest in all Japan. Murakami credits Ishiwatari, who had studied at the Ritz in Paris, with bringing to Japan a style of food service that set standards still maintained today.

In cooking, the basics are most important. Never compromise on the basics.

As a young man starting out at the Imperial, Nobuo Murakami earned the sum of 4.5 yen per month—this, at a time when a bowl of noodles cost nearly one-fifth of a yen. Salary levels in those days were outrageously inequitable. Top chefs were paid very well, but the rest of the kitchen staff barely at all: they had to pool tip money in order to have cash for food. Murakami lived with two friends in a small six-mat room (rooms in Japan are still measured by how many standard-sized tatami mats of 5.8 by 2.9 feet fit on the floor), splitting the rent of 13 yen per month three ways. The work day was from 6:00 A.M. to 11:00 P.M., with a break from 2:00 P.M. to 4: P.M. during which he would study. He was given two days off a month, and that was considered generous, since many Ginza restaurants gave only one day off a year. The most pressing problem the 18-year-old dishwasher had was that he didn't know how to cook—and no one was about to teach him.

In those days, chefs were every bit as temperamental as opera singers. They refused to share their secrets. Murakami would be told to start the preparations for potato salad, only to have the chef take over the finish. Backs would be turned to prevent prying eyes from uncovering the carefully guarded secrets of a mayonnaise.

It became clear that if he wasn't going to be *given* any training, Murakami would have to "steal" it. He tasted everything left in the pans to try to learn how things were made. But once the chefs realized they had an inquisitive dishwasher, they began adding salt and soap to the pans

in order to protect their treasured recipes.

Eventually, however, because he did such a fine job scrubbing out their pots, they stopped sabotaging his efforts to learn. Those tastes, and the culinary recollections of a friend's French uncle, were the only clues he had to reconstructing one of the world's most complex cuisines.

Murakami was intrigued by a dish that had been created in 1936 for the great opera star, Fyodor Chaliapin. Alas, the maestro—a dedicated carnivore—had dental problems during his stay at the Imperial. He asked Chef Tsutsui to prepare some meat that he would be able to chew, perhaps sukiyaki, which traditionally uses very thin, tender beef. Not content to serve anything that mundane to the great basso profundo, the chef grilled thin slices of beef and then marinated them with grated

Executive Chef Murakami making a point in the Fontainebleau kitchen.

onion. Naturally, he did this in a corner so that the other chefs couldn't see what he was cooking. The dish was a brilliant success and, thereafter, the singer ordered the same dish each time he came into the Grill. Tetsuzo Inumaru dubbed the dish "Chaliapin Steak." It still appears on the Imperial's menu.

Young Murakami wanted to recreate the dish that had received such immediate acclaim. Vainly, he sought clues by watching the chef as closely as possible. But his mentor always waited until he was out having lunch to tenderize the meat. One day, after leaving the kitchen for a break, Murakami pretended to have forgotten something and doubled back, hoping to catch Tsutsui in the act. But the kitchen door had been locked. The chef wasn't taking any chances. It was only when Murakami entered military service that the chef, thinking it was unlikely his apprentice would survive combat, finally revealed the secret of Chaliapin Steak (see recipe on page 126).

In the 1930's, 70 percent of the hotel's guests were American and the entire menu was in French and English. The young disciple not only had to learn how to cook, but how to read foreign languages. The hotel's repertoire comprised dishes he could not pronounce, no less had ever tasted. They were meant to please a palate largely untranslatable into his own experience. For starters, in Japanese cuisine there is no such thing as *rare*, *medium*, or *well done*. Meat is identified according to its method of preparation, i.e., grilled or broiled, and is always served at precisely the same very "Zen" point—when it is ready.

According to Murakami today, here is how to tell if beef is done: press it with your fingertip—if it feels like your cheek, it's rare; if it feels like your earlobe, it's medium; if it feels like the side of your nose, it's well done; and if it feels like the tip of your nose, it's very well done. He looks up and smiles. "The problem is that everyone's face feels different."

Returning to the Imperial after the war, the secret of Chaliapin Steak in tow, the young Murakami was saddened to find that he had been forgotten during his five-year absence. So many people had come and gone that the chef did not recognize him. Although he had been promoted from dishwasher to cook before the war, he had been on the lowest rung: cutting vegetables. Still, Murakami knew a way to identify himself. He picked up a knife and began chopping. As the rhythmic sound of his distinctive *rat-a-tat-tat* filled the kitchen, so did the smiles of recognition. Murakami was home.

No sooner was he back in stride than he was "loaned" by the hotel to the Japanese embassy in Belgium. Once again, the tables were turned. Murakami arrived in Brussels prepared to forge the rapids of classic French cuisine, only to find that he was expected to cook Japanese food—something for which his training at the Imperial had not prepared him.

A stint next at the Ritz in Paris brought the young cook back to classic French cuisine, and eventually home to the Imperial, where he began to create a unique culinary—and managerial—style that won him appointment as head chef for the Tokyo Olympic Games in 1964.

The Tokyo Olympics brought some 7,900 international athletes to town, hungry young competitors for whom dinner meant a lot more than a quiet table in the corner. Food was fuel. To solve the problem of feeding 10,000 people three times a day (coaches and journalists had to eat, too), the Olympic Committee invited Chef Murakami to attend the 1960 Rome

Olympics as an observer. "I was amazed," he said, "not by the extensive preparation required to feed so many people from different backgrounds, but at the sheer amount that the competitors ate." The first thing he had to do was readjust his concept of portions: athletes were eating twice as much as ordinary people.

Once back in Tokyo, Murakami made the rounds of embassies and consulates in search of national recipes and cooking tips. After preparing sample dishes, he'd send them to the embassies for comments. During this period, he organized a team of 300 cooks and 60 kitchen helpers, whom he trained to work in twelve cafeterias that were specially built for the Olympic Village.

"We were still considered a somewhat backward nation technologically, so we really had to prove ourselves," he recalled. "The French were concerned about the quality of Japanese fruit and vegetables. The Germans had to be convinced that we could make pumpernickel bread that would satisfy their tastes. I actually had to bake a few loaves and let the Germans sample them; otherwise, I think, they would have flown in bread from home. And some countries knew so little about Japan that they asked us if we had refrigeration!"

In discussing his career, Murakami recalls Tetsuzo Inumaru advising him that the best way to enhance his reputation was to write for the average Japanese housewife and not for other chefs. Inumaru was right. Soon women all over Japan began reading his books, and then watching "Dish of the Day" and "Window on Cooking"—as Chef Murakami, for twelve years on television, began unraveling the mysteries of classical French cooking.

Incredibly, he has never lost his perspective. When asked by some children during a school visit "What is the best food?" he replied that the best food was their mother's cooking. And when asked over a glass of champagne where he gets his ideas for new dishes, Chef Murakami barely hesitated. He quoted an old proverb. "Look back to be inspired for the future."

Imperial Restaurants

"We invite our patrons to think
of our restaurants as a stage,
with each fine meal a performance."

—*Executive Chef Nobuo Murakami*

ésar Ritz is credited as the first to have recognized that fine food and service were prerequisite to the success of a hotel. He began a lifelong affiliation with the great Auguste Escoffier, whose international fame evolved solely from his work as a hotel chef. Similarly, from the time it opened its doors, the Imperial has given food service priority status. Discerning Tokyoites wanted to sample this new Western style of eating—sitting on chairs and eating meat in a room filled with strangers. The Imperial soon found itself in that most enviable of positions: the place everyone wanted to see became the place in which to *be* seen. With consummate skill, the hotel turned notoriety into prestige.

Today, the Imperial has no hotel dining room per se; instead there are fourteen highly individual restaurants and seven lounges and bars. Travelers are advised to check all former prejudices against "hotel food" at the door.

Unlike the stereotypical hotel restaurant in which guests find themselves surrounded by other guests, the Imperial's reputation as a power base attracts a cosmopolitan clientele: one is truly dining *out* in Tokyo rather than dining *in* a Tokyo hotel. The proof of this particular pudding is found in the Imperial's annual sales figures: the hotel earns more from its restaurants than its accommodations.

In response to the growing sophistication of travelers, the Imperial invited onto its premises some of the finest Japanese chefs to be found in the country. By positioning a select group of "tenant" restaurants to serve Japanese and Chinese cuisine, the hotel is able to offer its guests a range of culinary options on a level of excellence that is second to none. A rule of thumb for purists is to eat a national cuisine only within the borders of that nation. They claim, for example, that there can be no true Italian food outside of Italy. However limiting a point of view, it is based upon two valid presumptions: (1) only locally farmed ingredients (tomatoes grown near Sorrento versus those grown in England) produce authentic taste; and (2) native chefs cooking for fellow countrymen do not adjust recipes to foreign palates. Soil and technique work in tandem. The argument is not without merit. How else to explain the glories of the American hamburger, Chinese dim-sum, Swiss fondue, or Hungarian goulash?

How else to explain Japanese food in Japan? If there is one cuisine about which the purists are right, it is Japanese. Other great cuisines reflect the societies from which they emerged: Chinese wok cooking is based upon a scarcity of fuel; French is a peasant cuisine that dreamed of being King; American is a cuisine of plenty. Japanese food expresses far more than the social conditions under which it developed or the resources that were available. During centuries of relative stability and nearly total isolation, it reached deep into the hearts of its people for inspiration. It emerged as the most formal of all cuisines, but is, paradoxically, the least restrictive. It is cerebral, artistic, sensual, honest, and demanding.

Japanese food is to Tokyo what the waltz is to Vienna, the Impressionists to Paris, the Bolshoi to Moscow. Each meal is a creative experience to be savored with the eye as well as the palate. Round food is served on square plates—round plates are reserved for square food. There is virtually no such thing as a matching service in the Western sense: it would be far too limiting. Indeed, many serving pieces are priceless artworks or else have been created specially to enhance certain foods. And always there is something on the plate to remind one of nature—a red maple leaf, a pine needle, or a flower.

It is a highly stylized cuisine that reveres both flavor and presentation. The elements are put together not merely for how they taste but for how they look. The diner is put on notice: he is there to experience more than one type of nourishment.

Tied to the ocean and the land, and the expectations of the palate, Japanese food is the one thing Japan hasn't quite figured out how to export. Sushi in New York is like New York pastrami in Paris and soup à l'oignon in Rio: it just doesn't translate. The purists are right. East is east.

But west is not always west. The twain met when the French came to Tokyo. They came, they saw, they cooked. After centuries of defining for the world what is sauce for the goose, the French began to deglaze their own preconceptions. They examined the aesthetic plating of dishes as intensely as van Gogh examined the works of Hiroshige. They noted the unusual combinations, the preference for natural essence rather than enriched sauces, the lack of dependence on herbs and spices, even salt and pepper.

Not content with a mere flash in the pan, the French decided to change all the ground rules. They declared "nouvelle cuisine" the new standard. Followers fell into place. Trend watchers quickly added another notch to their belts.

Although it has taken years for the world to develop a culinary nostalgia for classic French food, thanks to the devotion of Chef Murakami and the Japanese respect for tradition, dishes that are suddenly back in vogue on the rue de la Paix were never off the menu at the Imperial. As the song says, "Everything old is new again."

LA BRASSERIE

Instant Left Bank. Black and white ceramic tile floors that echo the tinkling of glass and the clatter of silverware. Oak wood paneling, brass railings, and mirrors, mirrors, mirrors. Tufted *vin rouge* banquettes. Art nouveau chandeliers. A restaurant where laughter is contagious, and conversations (like the scent of freshly baked bread) waft uninvited but welcome from table to table.

Are you absolutely sure that isn't Cézanne sitting across the room?

The decor flatters everyone: Those casually dressed appear world-weary; the modish drip sophistication. The clientele looks smart enough to belong to the Mensa Society, as does an even more exuberant group of waiters than those who said hello to Dolly at the Harmonia Gardens. This place is fun. Never rushed but always lively. Too much fun perhaps to discuss a new business plan.

No, that couldn't possibly be Cézanne.

Brasseries first sprang up in Paris around the turn of the century when Alsatian brewers sought convivial outlets in which to promote their beers. They introduced what has become classic "brasserie" cuisine—dishes hearty enough to stand up to the best of their frothy brews: choucroute, quiche Lorraine, veau Normande and an onion soup made from a 24-carrot broth. Recreated by the Imperial at the suggestion of president Ichiro Inumaru, the Brasserie is the latest link in the hotel's Tokyo-Paris culinary connection.

The waiter puts a silver stand in the middle of a table. He tops it with a tray of crushed ice on which a dozen sweet, not briny, Matoya oysters from Mie Prefecture lie defiantly undressed. No one even acknowledges the Sauce Mignonette. Nowhere is the mix of Japan and the West

Lunchtime at La Brasserie.

The Rainbow Room buffet, with views toward the Imperial Palace.

more striking than at a table in the Brasserie. Three stylish Japanese women, all wearing hats, linger long enough over the iced seafood platter for their steak frites to arrive. Then, as if having a picnic lunch, they take some beef, some oysters, some frites—ignoring the artificial confines of hors d'œuvres and entrées.

Rosy-faced Brits in the corner quaff beer while digging into plates of grilled sausages. A young American couple, still intently reading their Kabuki programs, try to piece the plot together over omelettes and a half-carafe of wine. No one notices they have begun to argue. The Brits are laughing out loud. And that man across the room who looks so familiar has ordered the confit.

Perhaps he is Gauguin.

RAINBOW ROOM

Where to look first? Panoramic views of Tokyo compete with heroic buffets at breakfast, lunch, and dinner. The buffet wins.

A huge, open space with banquettes and well-separated tables, the decor is a calming blend of pink, orange and mauve. Glass partitions reflect the cityscape, making it visible even with one's back to the windows. The raised floor in the center of the room has three buffet stations (cold dishes, hot dishes, desserts)—and lots of hungry Tokyoites. In 1957, after returning from a Scandinavian trip, Tetsuzo Inumaru sent Chef Murakami (who was in Paris training at the Ritz) off to Stockholm for a crash course in Swedish buffet. As a result of those trips, the Imperial opened a smorgasbord restaurant in 1958 to challenge the concept that less is more. Equally challenging were efforts to pronounce "smorgasbord," a tongue-twister in any language but nearly impossible in Japanese. Hollywood to the rescue. A film titled *The Vikings* was being shown in Tokyo at the time. The restaurant was named after the film and the word "Viking" translated itself into Japanese as a generic term for smorgasbord.

If ever a restaurant were all things to all people, it is the Rainbow Room. Tables are filled with ladies who lunch, men who EAT, and couples for whom the room's luxury liner mood seems to guarantee a shipboard romance. At night, with the lights of Tokyo dominating the room, even the aspic seems to sparkle.

Look carefully: The ladies' lunch plates are dotted with tiny portions of steamed fish and salads that wouldn't fuel a guppy. But taking more at one time wouldn't allow them to pair off and go back to the buffet for curried chicken, pasta bolognese, and beef stroganoff—all the while savoring a delicious bit of gossip. Alternating tastes and trivia, they are satisfied on all counts. The data processing pros at the next table, plates piled high with thick slabs of roast beef, stalk the buffet by themselves. They are hunter-gatherers who bond only after the entrée.

No matter the internal leitmotif—social, business, or romance—the ambiance of the room is contagious. Buffet dining has always been associated with a celebration. The party at the Rainbow Room never ends because after dinner one has only to cross the hallway into the Rainbow Lounge. It is an even more spectacular space for having a drink or a dance while soaking up the surrounding vistas of Tokyo.

LES SAISONS

The season at Les Saisons is always spring. This is a room that has never felt a chill in the air, let alone even heard of winter. Intensely romantic, it is a room of decorative moldings and floor-to-ceiling columns, overstuffed orange paisley sofas, white wicker, palm plants, and windows with three layers of diaphanous curtains. It is a restaurant in which women feel feminine and men feel masculine because the decor does not emphasize gender but youth.

One's entrance to Les Saisons is carefully orchestrated—there is no way to walk through the vestibule without being stopped by the extravagant floral bouquet that dominates the space: it is Vivaldi translated into flowers. A pause to adjust the inner clock. Indirect lighting on tones of peach and apricot make it appear as though sun is streaming through the silk-draped windows. Even at night.

View from the Rainbow Room over Hibiya moat, toward the Imperial Palace.

Lunch at Les Saisons.

The room is filled with well-dressed people enjoying the perks of civilization. The most soignée diner cannot help but be impressed as six waiters, using both hands, simultaneously lift the silver cloches from the plates of a dozen men in blue suits to reveal *millefeuilles de saumon fumé au caviar*—layers of crisp pastry circles sandwiching smoked salmon, topped by a dollop of caviar and floating upon the gentlest of tomato coulis. Lightly sautéed fresh foie gras is served with thin threads of sweet-sour red cabbage. The food is no less stylish than the decor, no less youthful.

The room may look French country-style but the menu is definitely city, and the city is Paris. Very Right Bank. Each place setting is fitted with different patterns of Limoges as variations on a theme. There is a witty glass-walled gazebo, a charming fantasy fashioned with a tile floor and white wicker chairs. It heightens the sophisticated edge of a room filled with sparkling crystal and gleaming silver.

Around an imaginary corner, behind a glass screen that gives the illusion of privacy but not isolation, a young maitre d'

Les Saisons table setting features the plates depicting the four seasons. Clockwise from front: Spring; Winter; Fall; Summer.

composes a steak tartare as though he were Mozart. A large dessert cart glides silently across the carpeted floor to a pair of Australian investment bankers on retainer for their foresight but who cannot decide between the hazelnut ice cream or the chartreuse soufflé.

PRUNIER

Cool, white marble upholstered banquettes. Burnished mahogany walls. A masculine setting in which women blossom like desert flowers. The room is very "clubby." Sedate. Reeking with power. CEOs to the right, CEOs to the left. The maitre d' rolls a cart over, displaying the catch of the day. An otherwise well-mannered finger points. The maitre d' nods his approval. Then he asks, "Boiled? Baked? Poached? Or grilled?" It is the closest mere mortals will come to having their own cooking staff.

To that end, Prunier uses an open kitchen gleaming with copper and the starched whites of a team of chefs who carry on traditions begun at Madame Prunier's renowned fish restaurant in Paris. In 1929, again seeking to expand its culinary vocabulary, the Imperial sent chefs to study there. The lessons they learnt then are still practiced today: Offer only the finest, freshest fish, and prepare it to taste.

One watches the cooks—it is almost impossible not to, since they are watching back—keeping time with the table's pace so that the next course will be ready at precisely the right moment. Their high white toques bob up and down like punctuation marks highlighting the action in the room. As busy as the open kitchen is, the restaurant is a sea of calm, light years from the rough and tumble "fish house" atmosphere to which Westerners are accustomed.

At a secluded table in the corner, a young

Prunier—the elegance of marble and the theater of an open kitchen.

woman (is she his daughter or his second wife?) smokes a black cigarette between taking bites of crisply fried whitebait that are piled on her plate like matchsticks. Across the room, a Russian and a Japanese are both speaking English. One opts for a latticework of salmon and sole in champagne sauce, the other for a filet of Kobe beef. A triumph of détente. The room is charged with an undercurrent of politics, business, diplomacy, and braised prawns rolled in cabbage. Instead of romance, one inhales the scent of seduction found in places of power.

Sitting at stage center, in burgundy velvet armchairs, is an elegant French couple. Dom Pérignon in the ice bucket. Crisp rolls untouched. He savors a forkful of tomalley (the lobster's "foie gras") while she deftly uses chopsticks to coax pieces of devil fish off its frame. An entire creature has been deep fried—mouth wide open and angry, its tail curled as a base so that the fish seems caught in midair. Devil fish is not on the menu. She dips a nugget of its moist white flesh into a light lemon sauce. One cannot help wondering how she knew what to order. A definition of power.

FONTAINEBLEAU

Ruby-red velvet walls, crystal chandeliers, the soft tinkle of a piano. Elegance with comfort. This jewel in the Imperial's culinary crown recreates the opulence of a bygone era. Aperitifs are served in a small, cozy lounge where one lingers over the menu and selects dinner. All the while, a pianist plays the way Piaf sang. She wears a simple silk blouse, drips strands of pearls, and is sheathed in a long black skirt as though just stepping out of a thirties movie. Then the flutist appears, a young woman in a white gown with tiny silver sequins. Together they play *Melody in F*. A Buddhist monk, perhaps recalling a previous life, smiles to himself as he table hops. Four stylishly dressed young Japanese women, flush from shopping, park their Wako and Chanel packages in the corner as one would park a Mercedes when scorning ostentation. A waiter leans over their table to strike a match. This is a room in which waiters still light women's cigarettes and in which women still enjoy the attention. The next musical selection is *Traumerai*. What year is this?

Named after the palace in which the Roman-numeraled Louis' frolicked, this is the French restaurant of everyone's personal *recherche du temps perdu*. It echoes the traditions of *haute cuisine* as well as a style of service that has all but disappeared in today's bottom-line world. Most of the tables in the dining room are filled with couples. One is set with flags for a diplomatic party. At another, there is a Japanese woman, alone, the dowager empress of some deeply personal domain. She wears a black beaded gown, very blue eyeshadow, and eats a dozen raw oysters with as much relish as if she had caught them herself. Quite comfortable with her own company, thank you very much.

Executive Chef Murakami discussing the menu with two regular patrons of his monthly gourmet evening.

Arriving at one's table, sinking back into a blue brocade armchair, the light gently filtered through frosted-glass lamps, extravagance suddenly becomes necessity. Each table has its own staff of three: a waiter who brings the platters from the kitchen to the cart; the maitre d' who plates the food; and a second waiter who brings the plate to the table. The magic of Fontainebleau is that one is almost convinced there is no other way to survive.

And then the first taste of *foie gras de canard* or *oeuf poche Alexandre* confirms it.

TOKO-AN

Sado is the word for the aesthetic sensibility behind the unique Japanese tea ceremony that is meant to inspire mutual respect and closeness among its participants. Invented by Zen monks to help keep themselves awake during long periods of meditation, the ceremony was formalized as an art form by tea master Sen-no-Rikyu in the sixteenth century.

One arrives at Toko-an (its name means "the sun is ascending into the heavens") as though entering a time warp. A glass wall looks out onto a fully landscaped Japanese garden that ignores the reality of being on the fourth floor of the Imperial Hotel. Designed by Togo Murano, an expert on *sukiya* (teahouse) architecture, the setting succeeds as much by its use of natural materials such as stone, wood and paper as it does by tradition. Murano has reinterpreted classical principles of architecture to create a modern yet authentic design. The purpose of a teahouse is to create a sense of inner peace, and the ceremony begins the moment you walk along a carefully arranged path of stones (*roji*) that has been sprinkled with water as a sign of welcome. The "dewy path" is the route along which one sheds the cares of the outside world.

The main chamber of the teahouse measures four and a half tatami mats, according to the traditional Japanese system for determining room size. The tearoom is sparsely decorated with only a flower arrangement or an ink painting intended as a miniature of the world in harmony.

After you take off your shoes, step up into the tearoom, and sit on the tatami mat, you will be served a small sweet on a piece of paper. The hostess then begins the tea service. Her stylized hand movements are designed to promote clarity and tranquillity of mind. It is a very precise performance, but not one meant to be solemn. The ritual is to be experienced with enjoyment, not awe. Following a sequence used for generations, she folds a silk cloth and wipes the utensils, signifying purification. She pours hot water into a bowl to warm it and then dips a new whisk into the water to soften its bamboo tines and make them more flexible.

Powdered green tea is put into the bowl, then hot water, and it is whisked until the tea becomes frothy. The hostess turns the bowl so that the front side faces you. She bows slightly. Your tea is ready.

The incredible artifice of each hand movement draws you away from the outside world. Your field of focus narrows to the curve of a finger, the arch of a wrist. Without your realizing why, they are suddenly as impressive as the tallest building or the longest bridge. A bite of the sweet (*wagashi*), a sip of the bitter tea (*matcha*), and one has experienced a basic element of the tea ceremony—a balance of taste.

The path leading to the tea house. Its name, Toko-an, is depicted on the wall in characters read from right to left. Directly translated, the characters would read "East Shining Hut." *Right*, interior of Toko-an.

Isecho—a waitress sets a place at a low table in the Japanese-style room.

ISECHO

Nearly 300 years ago in Kyoto, Iseya Chobe opened a restaurant that soon became synonymous with the best in Japanese cuisine—tea ceremony cooking. *Kaiseki ryori* follows guidelines established by ancient tea masters who served only the finest seasonal foods presented on dishes selected to complement the fare. To disciples of Zen, simplicity and serenity were of paramount concern: A *kaiseki* meal was defined as one that pleased the eye as well as the palate. After adhering to those demanding principles, Isecho (an abbreviation of its founder's name) began catering to the imperial household, an honor that has lasted through the centuries.

The decor of Tokyo restaurant to which they have brought their Kyoto cuisine is dramatic: black marble, sleek lacquer finishes. Delicate and expensive works of art provide a timeless elegance befitting the cuisine of emperors—there are serving cups valued at $4000 each. More traditional diners, however, may select a tatami-matted room that offers privacy amid more typical surroundings.

Not that anything at Isecho is typical.

The restaurant offers a full range of fare from sashimi to *shokado* (lacquered boxes filled with the world's most beautiful hors d'oeuvres). *Horakuzen* is one of Isecho's signature dishes in which fish, seafood, mushrooms, ginkgo nuts, green peppers, and lily buds are steam-cooked in a covered earthenware pot lined with sea salt. Pine needles are added for aroma. The result is perfection.

KITCHO

The word Kitcho means "eternal happiness," and *kaiseki*, the tea-ceremony cuisine that is the root of Japanese cooking and entertaining, means "warm stone." Originally such stones were used as hot-water bottles by Zen monks to comfort their empty stomachs during long periods of meditation. This is an appropriate introduction to Ishiyaki, a stunning dish in which a sizzlingly hot stone is presented in a basket filled with salt. One places paper-thin slices of raw shrimp and onion on the stone to cook. A splash of fresh lemon juice

Kitcho—Ishiyaki-style shrimp with a selection of sashimi.

is all that's needed to enter a delicious state of *kitcho*.

The main dining room is deceptively simple for a restaurant capable of complex artistry. Shoji screen walls, light wood tables with circular center panels that lift off to reveal cooking elements for preparing shabu-shabu and sukiyaki. Discreetly placed mirrors near the ceiling hint at space going into space, a nod to the floating world of ukiyo-e.

But the focus at Kitcho is on the world within the rim of a plate. Details of presentation run the gamut from a bowl made of seaweed (*kombu*) heated over wooden briquettes in a wire mesh basket, to the finest Imari, to a bamboo mat covered with a maple leaf. Delving even deeper, one finds a small salad garnished with one perfect *half* of a nut and cannot help but marvel at a cuisine that finds such passion in precision.

That most elusive of Japanese offerings, dessert, arrives in a hammered silver dish. A crystal clear wedge of fruit gelatin jeweled with pieces of fruit. It is the most elegant of *gelées*, pure shimmering velvet. On one side a cream sauce, on the other side kiwi. True *kitcho*.

TEN–ICHI

Legend has it that the Japanese learned to make deep-fried fish in the sixteenth century from Portuguese missionaries, who couldn't eat meat on Friday. But not until one has witnessed first-hand the dazzling Japanese translation of deep-fried is it really clear what tempura is all about. The best place to learn is at Ten-ichi, "The House of Tempura," one of Japan's oldest and most famous restaurants.

There is an air of conviviality at Ten-ichi that immediately puts one at ease. Check your Zen at the door and substitute impeccable for elegant, exuberant for intense.

Ten-ichi—the chefs serve the tempura while it's still sizzling.

Don't sit anywhere but at the bar, as close to the tempura master as possible so that you can watch him in action. A tempura service might begin with shrimp, then course-by-course with a single fish, mushroom, scallop, asparagus, etc. Each is presented in a procession guaranteed to raise the consciousness of even the lowliest onion. In case you're wondering, the chef uses discreetly placed grains of rice to keep track of how many pieces have been served.

The secret to tempura cooking is the ratio of sesame oil to salad oil—a carefully guarded formula that changes according to weather and temperature. Another secret is the flour: Ten-ichi has its own factory mix a special blend. Astonishingly, tempura batter is not prepared in advance. The chef uses a wire whisk to mix the eggs and ice water, and then chopsticks to incorporate the flour—he doesn't want too smooth a batter. And it must never get warm. No measurements, either. It is prepared according to feel—which is why tempura masters often make their own chopsticks.

Peking—semi-private room showing the cut-glass panel on the right.

PEKING

Of all the world's cuisines, the one that travels best is the rice-based cooking of China. No matter where: New York, Paris, Rome, Frankfurt, Nairobi—there is always a Chinese restaurant for a change of taste. An endless variety of dishes, as well as their unique methods of preparation, have enabled Chinese cooks in every country to translate regional specialties regardless of the limitations of local resources. Fortunately, the chef at the Peking restaurant has no such problem. In Japan, where the national passion for quality even exceeds the legendary French mania for fresh ingredients, Peking-style cooking can only be enhanced.

The setting is perfect. A hexagonal marble arch leads into a gray and sea-green room with etched glass panels that create an illusion of 1920's Art Deco. The menu is no less heroic than the entrance: nearly 200 dishes. What a joy of excess to select from six different preparations for abalone, nine for shark's fin.

One might begin with an hors d'oeuvre plate of smoked ham, chicken, and threads of crunchy jellyfish. In season there is "Three-Treasure Soup," a bird's nest broth with bits of sea urchin and the rare (and costly) Japanese *matsutake* mushroom. Deep-fried crab claw arrives with a crisp coating that surrenders to the flaky white flesh with which it has been stuffed. Still tender, perfectly cooked shrimp are blanketed in a spicy red sauce that owes its heat to Szechuan-style cooking. A dish of sautéed beef and vegetables is respectful of each ingredient—no one overpowers another.

During months without *matsutake* in them, have soup in the Chinese style—at the end of the meal. The Peking, predictably, offers 17 from which to choose.

NAKATA

One doesn't need a menu at a sushi bar, one needs trust. The first two or three items suggested by the Sushi Master are star turns selected to establish his credentials, making it more desirable, albeit more expensive, to sit at the counter than at a table, where fixed meals have set prices. At the counter, the level of extravagance is between you and your sushi master. Comparable to the camaraderie of a corner pub, good conversation with the man behind

Nakata's chefs making and serving sushi.

the bar enhances one's enjoyment of very recently deceased uncooked sea creatures served atop rice that has been moistened with sweet rice vinegar.

The only thing better than having a good conversation with the sushi master is not being able to converse at all. Suddenly, he becomes a career diplomat, a gracious host eager to please an honored guest. Because most sushi masters spend ten years in training, they are consummate professionals in a unique type of performance art. The knives are devilishly sharp. Barely missing his fingers, or so it appears, he slices fish with the precision of a diamond cutter dedicated to displaying the best facets of his skill. Watching him, one is suddenly distracted by the *absence* of something: the fish has no smell. The sea bream and tuna are too fresh to have developed any secondary scents.

If cleanliness is next to godliness, then Nakata is heaven. The unvarnished wood counter, the small crystal clear refrigerated cases that keep the fish at precisely the right temperature (never too cold), and the carefully selected tableware reflect the *Edomae* (old Tokyo) tradition as well as the purity of the fish itself.

The chef takes a handful of vinegared rice from the cooker, shapes it in the palm of his hand, and positions onto it a perfect slice of fish.

As it's presented, he speaks softly. "Arigato."

NADAMAN

*Man*suke *Nada*ya opened his first restaurant over 150 years ago in Osaka. At one time Osaka was the only city to compete with Kyoto for honors in *Kansai ryori*, the elegant haute cuisine of Western Japan. The Nadaman branch at the Imperial Hotel has been designed in traditional *sukiya*

Nadaman's summer bento.

(teahouse) style by Togo Murano, who is among the country's foremost classical architects. It is a perfect setting for one of the glories of Japanese dining—a traditional *bento* lunch.

Shokado is the name of the service in which food is presented in a beautifully lacquered box (*bento*) that has more surprises than an advent calendar. The *bento* is a veritable treasure chest filled with exquisite morsels of pumpkin, beef, vegetables, rice, *wasabi* (horseradish), rare *matsutake* mushroom or whatever else is in season or at peak freshness. Each ingredient has been selected to complement the other in taste, color, and texture. The great decorative arts of Japan are nowhere better exhibited than in a *bento* lunch.

Or in a slice of Kobe beef. Beer-fed steer are massaged by hand to marble ribbons of fat into the meat that the Japanese prize so highly that it is considered the ultimate gift. Ironically, no Western butcher would dare display Kobe beef in his counter for fear of a citation from the surgeon general. But since the Japanese eat meat rarely, they lavish their attention on producing the

Sushigen—a tuna steak, with various choices of sushi topping arrayed in the background.

behind a long cypress counter. They preside over prawns, fish and vegetables displayed on ice diamonds in a showcase as dramatic as any at Tiffany's. A truly handsome room of wood, leather, and tile, the menu here goes beyond sushi-bar fare into specialties such as tuna tartare. The chef shreds *toro*, the fattiest part of the tuna (a.k.a. the connoisseur's favorite), and blends it with cucumber, scallion, *nori* (seaweed), and a quail egg.

For those whose palates are not adventurous enough for sushi or sashimi (raw fish *sans* rice), Sushigen's repertoire includes a superb center cut of tuna broiled rare and accompanied by a mound of grated white radish topped with ground ginger and a splash of soy sauce. Daredevils may want to taste *anko* stew (made with the livers of angler fish) or chopped *anago* (sea eel) with rice and vegetables. The sushi master further demonstrates his respect for both customer and cuisine by braving the daily rough-and-tumble of Tokyo's legendary Tsukiji wholesale fish market where he must be tough enough to fight for top-quality fish.

For true comfort food, order *dobin-moshi*. Served in a small teapot, it is a soup for autumn made with *shimeji* mushrooms, red snapper, chicken, and ginkgo nuts. Open the top of the pot and inhale. Pour a small amount into a sake cup, add a squeeze of lime, and sip instant serenity.

world's best "special occasion" beef. The *sukiyaki* prepared at Nadaman sautées Kobe beef in an iron skillet, a simple and elegant way to experience this unique taste.

SUSHIGEN

According to one of Sushigen's chefs: "By using the edge of the knife vertically or obliquely, I can subtly alter the taste of the fish. This power of presentation is the essence of Japanese cuisine."

The essence of Sushigen (the Japanese characters mean: "fish," "great taste, and "quintessence") comes from the five chefs

OLD IMPERIAL BAR

This is no place for sissies. It is a man's bar, the kind Humphrey Bogart would have taken Ingrid Bergman to if he had made it out of Casablanca. It is a room that draws one in with its strength. It is not a bar for romance but for passion.

And make no mistake: Although there

are tables and banquettes around the room, deep leather armchairs that have supported the aching backs of overweight diplomats, gout-stricken shipping magnates, and prima ballerinas, this is a bar, not a lounge. There is a sleek, long, low counter, child-height hexagonal chairs in the Wright style, and a proper sloped edge for elbow-ing with the international set. Even when there are corner tables available, the bar is full. Simply, it is the best place to be. Over-head pin spots deliver reed-thin shards of light that blossom into circles on the mahogany surface. But first they catch a swirl of smoke from the blond woman in red listening intently to the Italian man in dark glasses. The bright white circles on the bar impart an almost cosmic fluores-cence to one's drink.

In a city dominated by progress and youth, the Old Imperial Bar is nostalgic even for those too young to remember. It is the closest one will ever come to the old Frank Lloyd Wright Imperial: a piece of an original mural, an oya-stone carved wall, the traditional hexagonal forms, the open latticework and brick, lots of leather and earth tones.

Amid the gently unobtrusive back-ground music, almost as remote as white sound, is the muffled crunch of a drink being shaken. The service area behind the bar is lowered so that the tuxedoed bar-tenders are almost at eye level. As though performing a military tattoo, only their arms and elbows move. They pour drinks as precisely as alchemists. Everything is

The Old Imperial Bar, featuring the original terracotta lattice-work from the Frank Lloyd Wright-designed Imperial Bar.

Drinks on the Old Imperial Bar. *From left to right*: Andersen Fizz; Bloody Caesar; Mt. Fuji.

measured by eye, yet proportions are always exact. There is no room for error: the Imperial Bar is consummately professional. Nothing has to be explained about "American" martinis or Moscow Mules. Come back twice and one is made to feel like a regular: a previous preference for olive or lemon is recalled, having been archived as conscientiously as one's blood type is in a hospital.

The man responsible for the bar that *Newsweek* has cited as one of the world's best is Takio Ito, who has been at the Imperial for 37 years. He began as a room boy, then a bar boy, then a bartender when the Old Imperial Bar was still the new Imperial Bar. It was, in those days, a standing bar, half a floor below the main lobby. There were ten or so tables, but habitués would stand at the bar to have their drinks. Martinis. Daiquiris. Whiskey sours. Cary Grant, Bob Hope, Jimmy Stewart. Ito recalls John Wayne: a big hand on a small glass of Cutty Sark.

Today, drinks are served in a spotlight. Nothing less would do.

MT. FUJI

1-1/2 ounces/40 ml dry gin
1 tbsp lemon juice
1/2 tsp pineapple juice
1/2 tsp sugar syrup
1/2 tsp cream
1 tsp maraschino liqueur
1/3 white of egg
maraschino cherry to decorate

Shake ingredients together in a cocktail shaker with ice. Pour into a chilled, saucer-shaped champagne glass. Decorate with a maraschino cherry on the side of the glass.

BLOODY CAESAR

1-1/2 ounces/40 ml Polish vodka
5 drops Worcestershire Sauce
2 drops Tabasco Sauce
celery salt
1 tsp fresh lemon juice
2 drops white wine vinegar
salt and black pepper
1 cup/250 ml chilled Clamato juice
1 stick celery or cucumber

Place 2 ice cubes in an 8 ounce/250 ml glass. Pour all the ingredients into the glass, adding the clamato juice last. Stir thoroughly. Decorate with a firm stick of celery or cucumber that can also be used as a mixer.

ANDERSEN FIZZ

2 ounces/60 ml Polish vodka
1 drop cream
1/2 lime, squeezed
1/3 egg white
2 drops Angostura bitters
1 tsp sugar syrup

Shake the ingredients together in a cocktail shaker, with ice. Pour into a 10 ounce/300 ml glass, with a few cubes of ice. Top up with soda water and blend.

Imperial Recipes

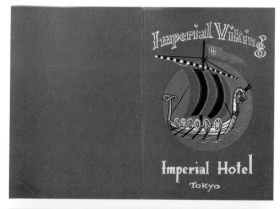

Salade Tiède de Langouste et Ris de Veau Vinaigrette au Curry

(Warm spiny lobster salad with sweetbreads and curry-flavored dressing)

LES SAISONS

Ingredients (Serves 4)

1/2 pound / 250 g sweet-breads

about 10 cups / 2.5 liters Court Bouillon (see recipe, p. 167)

juice of 1/2 lemon

4 live spiny lobsters or 4 lobster tails (about 1/2 pound / 250 g each)

1/4 pound / 125 g French beans

2 small bunches salad greens

1 Belgian endive

Curry Dressing:

1/2 tsp curry powder

1/2 tsp onion juice (see Note)

1/2 tsp Dijon mustard

1/4 cup / 60 ml white wine vinegar

3/4 cup / 180 ml salad oil

salt and pepper to taste

butter or salad oil for frying

Garnish:

1 tomato, peeled, seeded and diced

fresh chervil

diced truffle

Preparation time: Several hours

1) Soak the sweetbreads in cold water for several hours, changing the water when it becomes discolored. Remove the thin membrane with a sharp knife and trim off any bruised areas. Bring 4 cups / 1 liter Court Bouillon and the lemon juice to the boil. Add the sweetbreads, return to the boil, and cook for 3 minutes. Plunge sweetbreads briefly into cold water to firm, then drain on a linen towel and press between 2 cutting boards until cold. Slice thinly.

2) Place lobster in 6 cups / 1.5 liters boiling Court Bouillon and cover. As soon as bouillon comes back to the boil, remove cover and reduce heat. Simmer for about 4 minutes (longer if using frozen lobster tails). Check to see if the lobster is cooked by pulling away the shell of the chest cavity from the tail. If the soft green matter inside has solidified, it's ready. Drain well and split the shell. When cold remove the tail meat, and reserve heads and shells for decoration.

3) Wash French beans and then blanch in boiling salted water until just tender, not too soft (about 2 minutes). Drain the beans and plunge into cold water to preserve bright green color. Wash and dry salad greens, tear into bite-sized pieces. Separate endive leaves.

4) Curry Dressing:
Whisk together all the ingredients and warm gently in a double boiler.

5) To serve:
Place each lobster tail on a warmed plate. Arrange shells, vegetables and greens as in the photograph. Sauté sweetbread slices briefly in a little butter or oil until they change color. Place alongside lobster. Drizzle the warm dressing over just before serving and garnish with diced tomatoes, fresh chervil and diced truffle.

Note:
To extract onion juice, squeeze a finely grated onion through cheesecloth or a clean linen towel.

Millefeuilles de Saumon Fumé au Caviar

(Millefeuilles of smoked salmon with caviar)
LES SAISONS

Ingredients (Serves 4)

1 pound/500 g Puff Pastry
(see recipe, p.170)

Dressing:
4 tbsp lemon juice
6 tbsp olive oil
salt and pepper to taste
1 tbsp finely chopped onion
1/2 medium tomato, peeled,
  seeded, and diced
2 tbsp tomato juice

1/2 pound/250 g sliced
  smoked salmon
2 tbsp caviar

Garnish:
cream whipped with chives
dill
finely chopped chives

Preparation time: 30 minutes

1) Roll out the pastry and cut into 12 circles, 4 inch/10 cm in diameter. Prick with a fork and bake in a very hot oven (450°F/230°C) for 10 minutes. Cool on a wire rack.

2) Dressing:
Blend ingredients lightly with a whisk.

3) To serve:
Place a pastry round in the center of each serving plate. Place a single layer of smoked salmon and a little caviar on top. Repeat process and finish with a pastry circle. Garnish with caviar, whipped cream and dill. Spoon dressing around millefeuilles and surround the dressing with chopped chives.

Soufflé d'Oursin
(Sea urchin soufflé)
LES SAISONS

Ingredients (Serves 4)

Beurre d'Oursin:

4 tbsp/60 g unsalted butter, creamed

1/4 pound/125 g sea urchin roe, puréed in a blender or food processor

3 cups/750 ml heavy (double) cream

salt and pepper to taste

Soufflé:

1 egg yolk

1 cup/250 ml warm Béchamel Sauce (see recipe, p. 167)

1/4 pound/125 g puréed sea urchin roe (from 4 sea urchins; reserve shells)

2 egg whites

Garnish:

seaweed or salad greens

fresh chervil

Preparation time: 40 minutes
Cooking time: 10 minutes

1) Beurre d'Oursin:
Beat butter until soft. Beat in puréed urchin roe. Pour heavy cream into a pan and bring to a boil. Reduce heat, and simmer until reduced by 3/4. Gradually whisk in the butter and sea urchin mixture, a little at a time, to thicken the sauce. Season to taste. Keep warm in a double boiler.

2) Soufflé:
Grease 4 individual heatproof soufflé dishes. Beat egg yolk into the warm Béchamel Sauce. Heat gently (do not allow to boil). Remove from heat. Stir in puréed sea urchin roe and season to taste.

3) Beat egg whites until they form stiff peaks. Add 1 tbsp to the sauce. Fold in lightly with a metal spoon or spatula. Fold in remaining egg white, taking care not to over mix. Fill each individually prepared soufflé dish with the mixture. Place dishes in a preheated oven (400°F/200°C) and bake for 10 minutes.

4) To serve:
Top each soufflé with a little Beurre d'Oursin and serve garnished with seaweed and chervil. (Use salad greens if seaweed is not available.) Serve any remaining butter sauce in the reserved sea urchin shells. Serve immediately.

Foie Gras Frais Sauté sur Lit de Haricots Verts

(Sautéed fresh foie gras and young green beans)

LES SAISONS

Ingredients (Serves 4)

1 cup /100 g red cabbage, finely shredded

3 tbsp red wine

2 tbsp port

salt and pepper to taste

3 ounces /80 g very young green beans

butter for frying

1/2 pound /250 g fresh foie gras (goose or duck liver)

1 tbsp peanut oil

1/2 cup /125 ml Périgueux Sauce (see recipe, p. 169)

Garnish:

1 Belgian endive, leaves separated and washed

rock salt

mignonette

Preparation time: 20 minutes
Cooking time: 5 minutes

1) Blanch shredded red cabbage in salted boiling water to soften. Drain well. Sprinkle red wine on cabbage to add color. Mix in port and season with salt and pepper to taste.

2) Blanch whole green beans in salted boiling water for 2–3 minutes and drain. Sauté in a little butter. Season with salt and pepper to taste.

3) Clean and trim the goose or duck liver. Cut into 4 1/4-inch/6-mm slices and season well. Sauté foie gras in peanut oil until it's a rich brown.

4) To serve:
Arrange green beans in the center of each serving plate. Place a slice of foie gras on top and spinkle with rock salt and mignonette. Garnish with endive and red cabbage, spoon on the heated Périgueux Sauce and serve immediately.

Coquilles Saint-Jacques Espadon

(Curried scallops)

PRUNIER

Ingredients (Serves 4)

8 large scallops
salt and pepper to taste
12 mushrooms, thinly sliced
2 shallots, minced
1/2 cup/125 ml white wine
1 tbsp curry powder
2 tbsp/30 g butter
scant 1/2 cup/400 ml heavy (double) cream
from 1 to 1-1/2 cups/250–375 ml Hollandaise Sauce (see recipe, p.168)

Optional garnish:
1 tomato rosette
fresh parsley
wakame seaweed
puff pastry shells

Preparation time: 15 minutes
Cooking time: 2–3 minutes

1) Rinse scallops in lightly salted water. Drain and place in a pan, sprinkle with a pinch each of pepper and salt and place the sliced mushrooms and minced shallots over them.

2) Add the white wine, cover the pan and cook over high heat. As soon as the wine begins to boil, reduce the heat and simmer for 3 minutes. Remove from heat. Remove scallops and reserve.

3) Add the curry powder to the cooled liquid in the pan. Whisk in the butter, cream and Hollandaise Sauce. Do not reheat.

4) Place the scallops in 4 scallop shells, cover with the sauce, and place under a preheated broiler (grill) until golden brown. Garnish with parsley, tomato rosettes, *wakame* seaweed, and puff pastry shaped like shells.

Blanchailles Frites

(Deep-fried whitebait)
PRUNIER

Ingredients (Serves 4)

1 pound/500g whitebait (or other small fish, such as smelt or sardines)

3/4 cup/180 ml milk

salt and pepper to taste

4 cups/1 liter salad oil or olive oil for frying

1 cup/125 g flour

Garnish:

2 lemons

fried parsley sprigs

1 zucchini, thinly sliced

1/2 medium tomato, peeled, seeded, and diced

4 zucchini flowers

1 cup/250 ml Rémoulade Sauce (see recipe, p.168)

Preparation time: 15 minutes
Cooking time: 3 minutes

1) Just before frying, soak whitebait in milk for 3 minutes, then drain well and pat dry with absorbent paper. Season with salt and pepper. Preheat the oil in a medium-sized skillet (frying pan) until very hot (340°F/170°C).

2) Lightly dredge whitebait in flour, shaking off any excess. Deep-fry whitebait in the skillet a few at a time for 2–3 minutes, until golden. Remove with a slotted spoon and place them on absorbent paper to drain.

3) Serve immediately on heated serving plates garnished with lemon, parsley, zucchini slices, diced tomato and zucchini flowers. Pass Rémoulade Sauce around separately.

Œuf Poché Alexandre 1er

(Poached egg on brioche with caviar and smoked salmon)
FONTAINEBLEAU

Ingredients (Serves 4)

6 tbsp/100 ml milk

6 tbsp/100 ml Béchamel Sauce (see recipe, p.167)

2 tbsp sour cream

1 cup/250 ml Hollandaise Sauce (see recipe, p.168)

lemon juice to taste

salt and pepper to taste

4 medium eggs

2 tbsp white vinegar

4 slices of brioche or French bread (3-1/2 inches / 9 cm in diameter, 1/4-inch/6 mm-thick)

4 thin slices of smoked salmon

Garnish:

4 slices truffle

32 leaves mâche (lamb's lettuce)

about 2 ounces/50 g black caviar

Preparation time: 30 minutes

1) Add milk to the Béchamel Sauce. Warm gently over a low heat, stirring constantly, until mixture is heated throughout. Remove from heat. Stir in sour cream, 3 tbsp Hollandaise Sauce, a squeeze of lemon juice, salt and pepper to taste. Keep this sauce warm in a double boiler until ready to serve. (Do not reheat the sauce after adding the Hollandaise. It will separate.)

2) To poach eggs:
Heat slowly 4 cups/1 liter water to which the vinegar and 1 tsp salt has been added until simmering. Remove eggs from refrigerator just before poaching so egg whites will keep their shape. Break each egg into a separate bowl and slip them into the slowly boiling water, also one at a time. After the eggs have cooked for 3 minutes, remove each with a perforated spoon, quickly sliding each egg into a bowl of ice water to prevent overcooking. Drain, pat dry with absorbent paper and trim the excess egg white with a knife so that the eggs look as attractive as possible.

3) To serve:
With the back of a spoon, press a hollow into the center of each brioche or bread slice and warm briefly in the oven (do not allow them to change color). Place each slice of brioche on a warm plate. Top with a slice of smoked salmon.

4) Place eggs on a separate plate. Pour remaining Hollandaise Sauce over the eggs, with a spoon place an egg on each salmon slice, and top with a truffle slice. Place 6 leaves of mâche around each brioche slice; top each leaf with a little caviar. Spoon a little Béchamel Sauce mixture between the leaves and serve immediately. (If the Béchamel Sauce is still too thick, whisk in a little hot water).

Crème d'Avocat Glacée à la Bombay

(Iced avocado soup Bombay-style)
LES SAISONS

Ingredients (Serves 2–4)

1/2 small onion, finely chopped

1 tbsp finely chopped fresh ginger

2 tbsp/30 g butter

2 tbsp flour

1 tbsp curry powder

3/4 cup/180 ml clarified Beef or Chicken Stock (see recipe, p.166) or canned bouillon

1 ripe avocado

juice of 1/4 lemon

1/4 cup/60 ml light (single) cream

1/2 cup/125 ml plain yogurt

salt to taste

finely chopped chives to garnish

Preparation time: 30 minutes plus chilling time

1) Sauté the onion and ginger in the butter until slightly colored. Sprinkle with flour and curry powder and cook over low heat, stirring, for 1–2 minutes. Gradually add stock, stirring constantly and bring to the boil. Strain the soup, cool and refrigerate.

2) When the soup is cold, mash the flesh of the avocado with the lemon juice. Put through a sieve.

3) Stir the avocado into the cold soup together with the cream and yogurt. Add salt to taste. Serve in small chilled bowls with chopped chives sprinkled on top.

Soupe à l'Oignon au Gratinée

(French onion soup)

LES SAISONS

Ingredients (Serves 4)

- 1/4 baguette (French bread)
- 1-1/2 large onions, thinly sliced
- 2 tbsp/30g butter
- 1 tbsp flour
- 3 cups/750 ml clarified hot Beef or Chicken Stock (see recipe, p.166), or canned bouillon
- 1 cup/100g Gruyère cheese, coarsely grated
- salt and pepper to taste

Preparation time: 40 minutes

1) Cut bread into 1/8 inch / 3–4 mm thick slices. Toast very lightly, or leave out for several hours to dry.

2) Sauté onion slices in butter until golden but not brown.

3) Sprinkle the flour over the onions and continue to cook until mixture thickens. Gradually add the stock or bouillon, stirring constantly, and bring to the boil. Reduce heat and simmer for about 15 minutes over a low heat. Season to taste.

4) Pour soup into 4 heat-resistant ceramic bowls and cover the top with bread slices. Sprinkle with cheese and broil (grill) until the cheese has melted and is golden. Serve immediately with additional grated cheese if liked.

Bisque de Homard

(French lobster bisque)

PRUNIER

Ingredients (Serves 4)

1 live lobster (about 1 pound/ 500 g)

scant 1/2 cup/100 g unsalted butter

1 carrot, sliced

1 onion, sliced

3 tbsp cognac

6 tbsp white wine

salt and 5 peppercorns to taste

2 medium tomatoes, peeled, seeded, and diced

1 tbsp tomato paste

1 bouquet garni

1/4 cup/50 g rice

6 cups/1-1/2 liter Fish Stock (see recipe, p. 166)

6 tbsp cream

1-1/2 tbsp/40 g unsalted soft butter

2 tbsp cognac to taste

cayenne pepper to taste

chervil to garnish

Preparation time: 1 hour

1) Kill the lobster by piercing down the spine with a large knife. Remove the liver or tomalley (the dark greenish brown substance), and any orange roe, to use in flavoring the bisque. Cut lobster into several pieces.

2) Heat unsalted butter in a large pan and sauté vegetables over low heat for 5 minutes without allowing them to color. Add lobster pieces to the pan and sauté until they turn bright red. Pour in the cognac and ignite carefully with a match.

3) After flames die down, add white wine, peppercorns, a pinch of salt, diced tomatoes, tomato paste, bouquet garni, rice and Fish Stock. Bring the mixture to the boil, skim the surface and reduce the heat to a simmer. Cook for 30 minutes over low heat. Add more water as needed to maintain the level of liquid in the pot.

4) Remove bouquet garni and lobster from the pan. Remove meat from shell and discard shell. Dice meat into pieces about 1/2 × 1/2 inch (1 × 1 cm); reserve for garnish.

5) Strain the mixture in the pan and mash the vegetables and rice through a sieve. Return the purée and soup to the pan and heat gently, adding additional bouillon or water if the soup is now too thick. Add any reserved liver or roe. Gradually add the cream and softened butter bit by bit, beating constantly. Continue whisking until smooth. Season with salt and cayenne pepper.

6) Just before serving, add additional cognac to taste. Serve in individual soup bowls garnished with the diced lobster and chervil.

Potage aux Pêches Glacées

(Iced peach soup)

FONTAINEBLEAU

Ingredients (Serves 2–4)

2 large ripe peaches

2 cups/500 ml cold clarified Chicken or Beef Stock, (see recipe, p.166) or canned bouillon

1/2 cup /125 ml heavy (double) cream

1 tbsp Grand Marnier

1 tsp kirsch

juice from 1/2 lemon

sugar, salt, and pepper to taste

fresh mint to garnish

Preparation time: 10 minutes plus chilling time

1) Peel and pit the peaches. Purée through a sieve or blend in a food processor or blender until smooth.

2) Stir in the cold stock and cream. Add the Grand Marnier and kirsch, salt, sugar, and lemon juice to taste. Chill well.

3) Serve in chilled soup bowls garnished with sprigs of fresh mint.

Potage aux Huîtres à la Crème

(Cream of oyster soup)
FONTAINEBLEAU

Ingredients (Serves 4)

1/2 stalk celery

1/2 carrot

1/2 leek

1 small clove garlic, crushed

1 shallot, finely chopped

2 tbsp/30g butter

3 cups/750 ml Fish Stock (see recipe, p. 166)

1 generous pinch of saffron, soaked in hot water to cover

salt and pepper to taste

25–30 shelled oysters

1/2 cup/125 ml white wine

1 tbsp cornstarch (cornflour)

1/2 cup/125 ml heavy (double) cream

1 fully ripe tomato, peeled, seeded, and diced

chives to garnish

Preparation time: 30 minutes

1) Cut the celery, carrot and leek into very fine julienne (matchstick) strips.

2) Using a large pan, sauté the garlic and shallot in butter until they begin to change color. Add carrots, celery, and leek and cook until soft, about 5 minutes over low heat.

3) Stir in the Fish Stock, saffron, and the water in which it was soaked. Bring to the boil, add salt to taste, reduce heat and simmer for about 5 minutes, stirring occasionally.

4) Wash oysters, drain and put in a saucepan. Add white wine and bring to a boil. Simmer for about 5 minutes. Season to taste.

5) Strain liquid from the oysters and add to the soup. Dissolve the cornstarch in a little cold water, add to the soup and cook until mixture thickens, stirring constantly. Stir in the cream, the oysters and diced tomatoes and heat through. Pour into heated serving bowls and garnish with chives.

Gratin de Langouste à la Crème
(Spiny lobster gratin)
LA BRASSERIE

Ingredients (Serves 4)

2 large spiny lobsters

10 cups/2.5 liters Court Bouillon (see recipe, p. 167)

15–20 white mushrooms

2 tbsp/30 g butter

1/4 cup/60 ml cognac

1/2 cup/125 ml dry white wine

1/2 cup/125 ml heavy (double) cream

1 cup/250 ml Béchamel Sauce (see recipe, p. 167)

1/2 cup/125 ml Hollandaise Sauce (see recipe, p. 168)

1/2 cup/50 g Gruyère cheese, grated

salt and pepper to taste

Preparation time: about 1 hour
Cooking time: 2–3 minutes

1) Boil the lobsters in a large pot of Court Bouillon or salted water (1 tbsp salt to 4 cups/1 liter water). Use enough liquid to cover the lobsters. Allow 8–10 minutes per pound/500 g. Split the shells in half with a large knife and scoop out the meat, cutting it into bite-sized pieces. Scrub the shells clean, pat dry, and grease the insides of the shells with a little butter.

2) Halve the mushrooms, sauté in butter until their moisture evaporates (3 to 4 minutes), add lobster meat to pan, and season lightly with salt and pepper. Sprinkle with 1 tbsp cognac, light with a match, and ignite to evaporate the alcohol. Add the white wine and heat until nearly all the juices have evaporated. Remove from heat and stir in half the cream and about 4 tbsp Béchamel Sauce.

3) Add about 2/3 of the Hollandaise Sauce and the rest of the cognac to the cool mixture. Spoon the mixture into the lobster shells. Bring the remaining Béchamel Sauce to a boil, add most of the cheese, remaining cream and Hollandaise Sauce. Season to taste.

4) Pour this sauce over the top of the mixture in the shells and sprinkle with remaining cheese. Place under a preheated broiler (grill) or in a very hot oven briefly until the top is golden brown. Serve with sautéed spinach, grilled tomatoes and boiled spring potatoes.

Cœur de Filet de Bœuf Metternich

(Fillet of beef Metternich)

LA BRASSERIE

Ingredients (Serves 4)

1-1/4 pound / 600 g fillet of beef

salt and pepper to taste

Soubise:

about 1 pound / 500 g pork fat (trimmings from roasts, chops etc., or sheets of fat from your butcher)

1/2 onion, sliced and parboiled

1 cup/200 g rice, washed

2 cups/500 ml milk

1 shallot, minced

1/2 pound /250 g white mushrooms, chopped finely

1 cup/250 ml cream

4 slices white sandwich or fresh bread for croûtes

oil for frying

1/2 cup /50 g Gruyère cheese, grated

1 egg yolk, beaten

1 tbsp paprika

1 cup /250 ml Béchamel Sauce (see recipe, p. 167)

1/2 cup /125 ml Madeira Sauce (see recipe, p. 169)

Garnish:

Mixed vegetables, diced and sautéed

Preparation time: 40 minutes
Cooking time: 40 minutes

1) Rub salt and pepper into the fillet of beef and roast in a preheated hot oven (400°F/200°C) for 15–20 minutes. Set aside.

2) Soubise:
Line a shallow, ovenproof casserole with sliced pork fat. Place the parboiled onion slices, rice, and milk in a saucepan, and heat over a low flame, stirring constantly, until all the liquid is absorbed. Do not allow to boil.

3) Pour the rice mixture into the casserole lined with pork fat and cover the top with more pork fat. Cover the casserole and bake in a preheated hot oven (480°F/250°C) for 20 minutes. Remove the top layer of pork, and spoon out the soubise into a sieve and strain.

4) Sauté the shallot and mushrooms in butter until all the liquid has evaporated. Mix with the soubise, then add the cream and mix well. Season to taste.

5) Croûtes:
Remove the crusts from the bread slices and cut into rounds, slightly smaller than the beef fillet slices will be. Sauté in hot oil until golden then drain well on absorbent kitchen paper. (The croûtes may be toasted if preferred.)

6) To serve:
Place the croûtes in the bottom of a shallow ovenproof pan. Spread a little soubise over each croûte. Cut the fillet into 4 slices and place a slice of meat on each croûte. Spread the rest of the soubise over the meat slices.

7) Add half the grated cheese, the egg yolk and paprika to the Béchamel Sauce and mix well. Pour the Béchamel mixture over the beef, sprinkle with remaining grated cheese and bake in a preheated very hot oven (480°F/250°C) for about 5 minutes, or until browned. Transfer to heated serving plates and serve with Madeira Sauce and mixed vegetables.

Omelette Lorraine

(Lorraine-style omelette with cheese and bacon)

LA BRASSERIE

Ingredients (Serves 4)

12 medium eggs
1-1/2 ounces / 40 g bacon, diced
1-1/2 ounces / 40 g Gruyère cheese, diced
1 tbsp chopped chives
salt and pepper to taste
4 tsp butter

Garnish:

Pommes de Terre à la Lyonnaise (see recipe, p. 171)
1/2 pound / 250 g fatty bacon grilled
1-1/2 ounces / 40 g Camembert, cut into strips

Preparation time: 15 minutes
Cooking time: 20 minutes

1) Beat whole eggs with a fork or whisk. Add bacon, Gruyère cheese and chopped chives. Season with salt and pepper. Divide mixture into 4 equal portions.

2) Add 1 tsp butter to a heated greased frying pan; swirl pan so that melted butter coats the surface. Do not let the butter brown. Pour one portion of the egg mixture into the pan and stir continuously with a fork until mixture sets. Invert the pan and turn out the omelette, folded over, into the center of a heated platter. Keep warm while repeating process with remaining ingredients.

3) Serve immediately, garnished with Pommes de Terre à la Lyonnaise and grilled fatty bacon topped with Camembert strips.

Choucroute Garnie à l'Alsacienne

(Alsace sauerkraut casserole)

LA BRASSERIE

Ingredients (Serves 4)

1/2 pound/250 g salted beef tongue

1/2 pound/250 g fatty bacon

1 pound/500 g ham hocks

3/4 pound/375 g German-style sausages (frankfurters, knockwurst, etc.)

2 pounds/1 kg canned sauerkraut

1 medium onion, peeled and sliced

2 pounds/1 kg pork trimmings

3 bay leaves

1 tbsp juniper berries

about 8 cups/2 liters Chicken Stock (see recipe, p. 166)

4 small potatoes

1 carrot

1 zucchini

Dijon mustard

Preparation time: 10 minutes
Cooking time: 3 hours

1) Simmer beef tongue, bacon and ham hocks in hot water to cover, for 2–3 hours to remove salt, changing the water a few times. Add the sausages toward the end of the cooking time to heat through.

2) Wash sauerkraut in cold water and place in a deep pan with onion slices, pork trimmings, bay leaves and juniper berries. Add Chicken Stock to cover. Bring to a boil and simmer for 1 hour.

3) Peel the potatoes and carrot, and turn (cut into neat barrel shapes). Wash the zucchini and turn. Boil separately in salted water until just tender.

4) To serve:
Drain the cooked meats and thickly slice the bacon and tongue. Drain the sauerkraut and place in a large serving dish. Arrange the meats on top, add the vegetables, and serve with mustard.

Steak Tartare

("La Brasserie" Tartar steak)

LA BRASSERIE

Ingredients (Serves 4)

3/4 pound /375 g finely ground, very lean beef (preferably prime beef)

Dressing:
salt and pepper to taste
4 tsp Dijon mustard
2 tsp white wine vinegar
4 tsp olive oil
4 egg yolks, beaten
Tabasco sauce to taste
Worcestershire sauce to taste

Garnish:
4 tsp mashed anchovy fillet
4 tsp finely chopped onion
4 tsp sour pickle, finely chopped
4 tsp finely chopped parsley
4 tsp finely chopped capers
1 tsp cayenne pepper
24 leaves mâche (lamb's lettuce)
8 radish roses

Preparation time: 20 minutes

1) Dressing:
Whisk together salt, pepper and mustard in a bowl. Add vinegar and olive oil in a slow stream, whisking constantly. Mix in beaten egg yolks, Tabasco, and Worcestershire sauce.

2) Mix dressing with meat using 2 forks or your hands; shape into 4 round patties.

3) To serve:
Place a teaspoon of each garnish on individual mâche leaves. Place a meat pattie in the center of a serving plate and surround with garnish and 2 radish roses. Serve with rye bread or toast.

Noisettes d'Agneau Corolle de Courgettes et Tomates

(Medallions of lamb on a crown of tomatoes and zucchini)

LES SAISONS

Ingredients (Serves 4)

2 zucchini (courgettes)

4 tbsp/60 g butter

2 tbsp oil for frying

10–15 small tomatoes, peeled

salt and pepper to taste

1 cup/250 ml Lamb Stock (see Notes)

3 pounds/1.5 kg boned loin lambchops, about 1-1/2 inch/3.5-cm thick

1/2 cup/125 ml sherry vinegar or red wine vinegar

Garnish:

Châteaux turnips (see Notes)

fresh young thyme

Preparation time: 40 minutes
Cooking time: 10 minutes

1) Cut zucchini into 1/4-inch/5-mm slices. Heat half the butter and half the oil in a skillet (frying pan) and sauté for a few minutes until just tender. Drain and reserve. Cut the tomatoes into slices the same size as the zucchini.

2) Butter a shallow ovenproof casserole and arrange the raw tomatoes and lightly sautéed zucchini in the dish in overlapping slices. Sprinkle with salt and pepper. Sprinkle 1 tbsp of the stock over the vegetables to keep them moist and heat at 300°F/150°C for 7–8 minutes.

3) Trim the fat from the lamb chops to form medallions, season well. Heat the remaining butter and oil in a skillet (frying pan) and brown the medallions, about 5 minutes on each side. Remove, and drain on absorbent kitchen paper. Deglaze the pan juices with the sherry vinegar. Add the Lamb Stock, bring to the boil and strain. Season to taste.

4) To serve:
Slice each medallion in half and arrange in the center of a heated serving plate. Surround with overlapping zucchini and tomato slices and spoon around the pan juices. Garnish with turnips and thyme and serve.

Notes:
To prepare Lamb Stock, follow the recipe for Beef Stock (see p. 166) but use lamb meat and bones instead of beef.
To prepare Châteaux turnips, peel turnips and cut into very small barrels. Blanch in boiled salted water until tender. Drain well. Just before serving toss in hot butter until well coated.

Bifteck à la Chaliapin
(Beefsteak Chaliapin)
LES SAISONS

Ingredients (Serves 4)

4 rump steaks (about 1/4 pound / 120–150 g each)

juice from 1 small onion (see Note)

2–3 large onions, finely chopped

1/2 cup / 125 g butter

salt and pepper to taste

3 tbsp salad oil

parsley and watercress to garnish

An original Imperial Hotel recipe, created by the Imperial Hotel's chef for the opera singer Fyodor Chaliapin, who stayed at the Imperial in 1936.

Preparation time: 30 minutes
Cooking time: 5 minutes

1) Pound beef with a meat mallet or with the back of a heavy knife to flatten and tenderize it. Remove any tendons, and marinate it in the onion juice for an hour or so.

2) Sauté the finely chopped onion in all but 2 tbsp butter over low heat until transparent. Season with salt and pepper, and set aside.

3) Sprinkle salt and pepper on both sides of beef. Heat salad oil and remaining butter in a skillet (frying pan). Brown meat on one side over medium heat for 3–5 minutes, turn, and cook lightly on the other side for about 10 seconds. Arrange on a plate.

4) Return sautéed onion to the same pan and continue cooking until lightly browned. Season to taste, and arrange chopped onions over steak, flattening with a spatula. Make criss cross lines on each with the edge of the spatula. Sprinkle with finely chopped parsley and garnish with watercress. Serve with hash browns, sautéed fava beans, and glacéed carrots.

Note:
To extract onion juice, squeeze a finely grated onion through cheesecloth or a clean linen towel.

Aiguillettes de Canard au Poivre Vert et aux Galettes de Maïs

(Sliced duck with peppercorn sauce)

LES SAISONS

Ingredients (Serves 4)

2 ducks (about 5 pounds/2.3 kg each)

Sauce Poivre Vert:
1 onion, chopped
1 carrot, chopped
1 garlic clove, crushed
a pinch of thyme
1 bay leaf
2-1/2 cups/600 ml Veal Stock (see recipe p. 166)
2 tbsp/30 g butter
2 tbsp green peppercorns (fresh or canned)
salt and pepper to taste

Galettes de Maïs:
1 cup/125 g flour
1/2 tsp baking powder
2 small eggs
1-1/2 tbsp sugar
1/2 cup/100 g drained canned corn
salt and pepper to taste

Garnish:
Finely sliced carrot and zucchini (courgettes), blanched
Finely sliced truffle
Fresh chervil

Preparation time: 1 hour
Cooking time: 10 minutes

1) Bone the ducks, keeping breasts whole, and remove the legs. Reserve bones and legs for the sauce. Roast duck breasts in a preheated oven at 480°F/250°C for 5–10 minutes. Reserve and keep warm.

2) Sauce Poivre Vert:
Sauté duck bones and legs in a saucepan for 5 minutes or until the fat runs. Add chopped vegetables, garlic, and herbs, and continue to sauté for 2–3 minutes. Pour in Veal Stock, bring to a boil and simmer over low heat for 30 minutes until volume is reduced by 1/3. Remove from the heat and gradually whisk in the butter. Strain through a sieve. Add the green peppercorns and season to taste.

3) Galettes de Maïs:
Sift flour and baking powder into a bowl. Beat eggs with the sugar and gradually add to the flour, mixing well with each addition. The consistency should resemble that of pancake batter. Stir in corn and seasoning. Drop small spoonfuls of the mixture onto a heated, greased pan or griddle. When bubbles appear on the surface turn with a spatula to brown briefly on other side. Serve immediately.

4) To serve:
Cut the duck breasts in thin slices and arrange lattice-style in the center of 4 serving plates. Spoon the sauce around the duck and garnish with Galettes de Maïs, zucchini, carrot and truffle slices.

Filets de Sole Murat

(Fillets of sole meunière)
PRUNIER

Ingredients (Serves 2–4)

2 medium-sized tomatoes
salt and pepper to taste
about 1/2 cup /60 g flour
salad oil for frying
1 large potato
6 tbsp /75 g butter
5 artichoke hearts (canned artichoke hearts may be used)
4 sole fillets (3 ounces /80 g each)
1/2 cup /125 ml milk
finely chopped parsley to garnish
juice of 1 lemon
Beurre Noisette to serve (see Note)

Preparation time: 30 minutes
Cooking time: about 5 minutes

1) Slice tomatoes thinly and sprinkle each slice with salt, pepper, and flour on both sides. Brown on both sides in a little oil and reserve. Keep warm.

2) Peel and finely dice the potato and sauté in 1 tbsp butter until cooked through, about 5 minutes. Set aside and in the same pan sauté diced artichoke hearts in a little more butter until tender (about 5 minutes). (If using canned artichoke hearts, just dice and sauté briefly until heated through.)

3) Cut each sole fillet in half lengthwise to give 8 fillet strips in all. Dip each piece in milk and then flour, to coat lightly. Sauté the sole strips in remaining butter until golden, turning once. After turning the fillets, add potatoes and artichoke hearts to the pan. Season with salt and pepper.

4) Arrange tomato slices on a plate. Spoon the sole mixture on top, sprinkle with chopped parsley and pour on the lemon juice mixed with the Beurre Noisette.

Note:
To make Beurre Noisette, heat 6 tbsp/75 g butter over low heat until light brown. Add a little lemon juice to taste and pour over the sole immediately. Be careful not to burn the butter.

Suprême de Sole Bonne Femme

(Fillets of sole Bonne Femme)

PRUNIER

Ingredients (Serves 4)

- 1 leek (white part only), sliced
- 2 stalks parsley, finely chopped
- 2 tsp fresh thyme, or 1/2 tsp dried
- 2 tbsp peppercorns
- 2 bay leaves
- 3 cups /750 ml Fish Stock (see recipe, p. 166)
- 3/4 cup /180 ml dry white wine
- butter
- 8 skinless sole fillets (about 2 ounces /60 g each)
- 8 fresh white mushrooms, sliced
- 2 ounces /60 g onion, finely chopped

Sauce:
- 3 tbsp/40 g butter
- 1-1/2 cups /375 ml Hollandaise Sauce (see recipe, p. 168)
- 1/3 cup/90 ml heavy cream, whipped
- salt and pepper to taste
- lemon juice to taste
- 2 tbsp finely chopped parsley

Preparation time: 40 minutes
Cooking time: 2–3 minutes

1) Place the leek, parsley, thyme, peppercorns, bay leaves, and Fish Stock in a large saucepan. Bring to a boil and simmer over low heat for 20 minutes. Strain and add white wine.

2) Melt butter in a large pan and arrange sole fillets in a single layer. Sprinkle sliced mushrooms and chopped onion on top and add enough stock and wine mixture to cover fillets. Place buttered wax paper over the fillets and simmer over low heat for 7–8 minutes.

3) Sauce:
Carefully remove fillets from the pan with a wide spatula and keep warm. Boil the pan liquid for a further 5–7 minutes to reduce and thicken. Gradually whisk in the butter and remove from heat. Carefully fold in Hollandaise Sauce and whipped cream. Season to taste with salt, pepper, lemon juice, and parsley.

4) To serve:
Place fillets on individual heatproof plates and spoon the sauce over them. Put in a preheated oven (480°F/250°C) for 2–3 minutes until the surface is lightly browned. Serve immediately.

Rondelles de Langouste Hongroise
(Slices of spiny lobster with paprika sauce)
PRUNIER

Ingredients (Serves 4)

4 live spiny lobsters
4 tbsp sliced shallots
1 tbsp cognac
1 tbsp paprika
1/2 cup / 125 ml white wine
1/2 cup / 125 ml Fish Stock
  (see recipe, p. 166)
scant cup / 200 ml heavy
  (double) cream
1 egg yolk, beaten
1 cup/250 g Saffron Rice (see
  recipe, p. 170)

Garnish:
green leaf
shell butterflies
fresh orchids

Preparation time with rice: 1 hour (Without rice: 45 minutes)

1) Prepare the Saffron Rice

2) Kill the lobsters by piercing the spinal cord with a sharp knife (where the head joins the body on the underside). Heat butter in pan and sauté the lobsters until they turn red. Add the shallots. Pour cognac over the mixture and ignite. After the flames die down, sprinkle with paprika. Add the white wine and cook until liquid is reduced by 2/3. Add the Fish Stock and half the cream and cook, covered, for 15 minutes over low heat. Remove the lobsters and cool.

3) Reduce the sauce slightly. Slowly whisk in the remaining cream and remove from the heat. Add the egg yolk, stirring constantly, and season to taste.

4) When lobsters have cooled, remove the meat from the tails (and claws, if using American lobsters). Cut the meat into circular slices. Make decorative butterflies with the shells.

5) To serve:
Place Saffron Rice on 4 serving plates and arrange the lobster slices around it. Spoon the sauce around and serve garnished with a lobster shell butterfly and a fresh orchid.

Blanc de Turbot aux Pignes Mesclun de Céleri

(Grilled turbot with pine nuts and celery)

PRUNIER

Ingredients (Serves 4)

1 pound / 500 g turbot cut into 4 fillets

salt and pepper to taste

6 tbsp/40 g shelled pistachios

1/4 cup / 50 g shelled almonds

3 tbsp/20 g pine nuts

2/3 cup /125 g butter

1/2 pound/250 g celery stalks

radicchio (trevise)

1/4 pound /125 g spinach

juice of 2 lemons

Preparation time: 30 minutes
Cooking time: 5 minutes

1) Sprinkle the turbot fillets with salt and pepper. Chop the pistachios, almonds and pine nuts coarsely and spinkle over one side of the fish slices, pressing down well.

2) Place the turbot slices in a shallow pan generously brushed with some of the butter. Place under a preheated broiler for 5 minutes, taking care not to scorch the nuts. (The fish can be fried if preferred, but cook it on the uncoated side only.)

3) Cut the celery into julienne (matchstick) strips, parboil and drain. Wash and dry the radicchio and spinach. Tear into bite-sized pieces. Heat the remaining butter in a skillet (frying pan) and sauté the radicchio, spinach, and celery until just beginning to wilt. Transfer to 4 heated serving plates. Add the lemon juice to the butter in the pan and whisk together (without heating).

4) Lay the turbot fillets on top of the vegetables. Sprinkle with the butter and lemon juice mixture and serve immediately.

Côtelettes d'Agneau Poêlées au Confit d'Oignons et Champignons
(Grilled lamb chops with onions and mushrooms)
FONTAINEBLEAU

Ingredients (Serves 4)

12 lamb rib chops (about 1-3/4 pounds/800 g)

2 slices bacon (1-3/4 ounces/50 g)

2 garlic cloves

salt and pepper to taste

1/2 pound/250 g small white onions

2 tsp sugar

6 tbsp/75 g butter

3/4 cup/180 ml water

1/2 pound/250 g white mushrooms

2 tbsp chopped shallot

4 tsp salad oil

Jus d'Agneau (see recipe, p. 169)

Garnish:

16 okra, lightly boiled

4 tbsp julienne (matchstick) potatoes, fried until golden

fresh chives

8 cutlet frills

Preparation time: 30 minutes
Cooking time: 4 minutes

1) Trim chops if necessary, and pound to flatten slightly. Remove bone, excess fat, and gristle from 4 chops and cut them into medallions (reserve the others). Cut the 2 slices of bacon in half lengthwise, and roll one bacon strip around each medallion. Pin the bacon ends with a toothpick.

2) Peel garlic cloves and cut in halves. Rub garlic over both sides of all 12 chops. Season both sides of all chops with salt and pepper.

3) Peel small onions and blanch in boiling water for 2–3 minutes, then drain. Place in a small saucepan with the sugar, 2 tbsp/25 g butter, water, salt, and pepper to taste. Simmer, covered, for 15–20 minutes.

4) Cut the stems off the mushrooms. Wash mushrooms well and cut into quarters. Heat 2 tbsp/25 g butter in a pan and sauté mushrooms over high heat. When the mushrooms give off liquid, season them with salt and pepper and continue sautéing until liquid evaporates and mushrooms are lightly colored. Just before serving, add chopped shallots and heat briefly.

5) Heat 2 tbsp/25 g butter and the salad oil in a large skillet (frying pan) and brown all the chops over high heat, turning to cook both sides. Be careful not to overcook–the meat should still be pink inside–only cook for about 3–4 minutes. Place a cutlet frill on each chop and remove toothpicks from the medallions.

6) To serve:
Arrange one medallion and 2 chops on each warm serving plate. Spoon on some mushrooms and cover with julienne potatoes. Arrange onions, moistened with a little cooking juice, okra and chives around the meat. Spoon on some Jus d'Agneau and serve immediately.

Caneton Rôti à l'Ananas
(Roast duck with pineapple)
FONTAINEBLEAU

Ingredients (Serves 4)

2 tbsp/30 g butter
salt and pepper to taste
1/4 cup/60 ml salad oil
1 cup/250 ml clarified duck stock (See Chicken Stock recipe, p. 166, but use duck carcass instead of chicken)

Pineapple sauce:
1 fresh pineapple
1 tsp grated fresh ginger
juice and grated peel of 1 lemon
1 tbsp pine nuts
a few drops of cider vinegar
1 tbsp orange marmalade
1/4 tsp cornstarch, dissolved in a little cold water
2 ducklings, 2 pounds/about 1 kg each, cleaned

Optional Garnish:
1 fresh pineapple
cherries
fresh mint
parsley
1 cherry tomato
1 leek
1 truffle

Preparation time: 35 minutes
Cooking time: 15 minutes

1) Rub butter, salt, and pepper over the duckling, inside and out. Heat salad oil in an ovenproof pan. Place ducks in the pan, breast side down. Roast in preheated hot oven (400°F/200°C) for about 15 minutes (see Notes), basting with the oil occasionally, until the meat is brown. Set ducks aside in a warm place. Deglaze the roasting pan with the duck stock. Strain, adjust seasoning to taste and reserve.

2) Pineapple sauce:
Chop the fresh pineapple into small chunks and purée in a food processor or blender. Strain. Pour boiling water over the grated ginger and lemon peel. Strain, immerse briefly in cold water, and strain again. Boil pine nuts for 30 seconds. Strain.

3) Place the strained pineapple juice into a saucepan. Boil over high heat until reduced by half. Remove from heat and add cider vinegar and marmalade. Stir and return to the heat. Add the cornstarch and bring to the boil, stirring, to thicken it slightly. Add the grated ginger and lemon peel, pine nuts and a squeeze of lemon juice. Correct seasoning to taste.

4) To serve:
Carve the meat from one duck and arrange with the whole duck on a large serving platter. Garnish the whole duck with parsley, leek, a cherry tomato and a truffle. Garnish the duck slices with fresh pineapple, cherries and a sprig of mint. Serve with a selection of vegetables and pommes frites or chips. Reheat the pineapple sauce and deglazed pan juices and pass around separately.

Notes:
This cooking time produces very rare meat; if you prefer your duck to be well cooked allow 15 minutes per pound/500 g.
Use the carcasses from the roast duck to make a good quality duck stock and store in the freezer until required.

Escalopes de Veau et Ris de Veau à la Crème aux Truffes

(Veal scallops and sweetbreads with cream truffle sauce)

FONTAINEBLEAU

Ingredients (Serves 4)

2 veal sweetbreads (about 1/2 pound/250 g each)

8 veal scallops (about 1/4 pound/125 g each)

flour for coating

salt and pepper to taste

3 tbsp/40 g butter

salad oil for frying

a little white wine for deglazing

Sauce Suprême aux Truffes (see recipe, p. 170)

Garnish:

8 truffle slices

1/2 pound / 250 g cooked noodles, tossed in butter and cream

4 squash or zucchini flowers

4 braised cabbage leaves

Ratatouille Timbales (see Note)

Preparation time: Several hours
Cooking time: 5 minutes

1) Soak sweetbreads in cold water for several hours (change the water as it discolors). Blanch in boiling salted water for 5 minutes, then immediately plunge into cold water to firm. Drain sweetbreads and set on a cutting board. Wrap in a linen towel and weigh down with another cutting board for about 2 hours, then trim away membranes and any discolored portions. Cut each in half.

2) Lightly dredge sweetbreads and veal scallops with flour seasoned with salt and pepper, shaking off any excess. Heat the butter and a little salad oil in a skillet (frying pan) and sauté sweetbreads and veal scallops over high heat until lightly colored on both sides.

3) Remove meat from the pan and keep warm. Drain off oil from the pan and add a little wine. Heat, stirring constantly to deglaze the pan, add to the Sauce Suprême aux Truffes.

4) To serve:
Arrange one veal scallop and one sweetbread slice on a heated serving plate and top each with a truffle slice. Spoon Sauce Suprême aux Truffes around the meat and garnish with noodles, a squash flower, a cabbage leaf (rolled into a barrel shape) and a Ratatouille Timbale. Serve immediately.

Note:
To prepare Ratatouille Timbales, finely dice a little zucchini, eggplant, red pepper and a peeled tomato. Sauté together lightly in butter until just tender then press into very small well-oiled timbale molds.

Pigeonneaux Rôtis aux Lentilles Sauce Bordelaise

(Roast squab with lentils and Bordelaise sauce)

FONTAINEBLEAU

Ingredients (Serves 4)

1/2–3/4 pound/250–375 g dried green lentils

3-1/2 ounces/100 g bacon, diced

1 medium onion, peeled and studded with 2 cloves

salt and pepper to taste

3 tbsp/40 g butter

4 squabs, plucked and cleaned

4 slices of bacon

5 tbsp/60 g clarified butter

Bordelaise Sauce (see recipe, p. 170)

Garnish:

12 thin pastry rounds

finely sliced zucchini, tomato, and eggplant, sautéed

blanched spinach

fresh thyme

Preparation time: 2 hours
Cooking time: 14 minutes

1) Wash lentils well, picking out any grit or broken pieces. Place in a saucepan and add water to cover. Bring to a boil and reduce the heat to simmer. Add diced bacon and onion studded with cloves. Season with salt and pepper to taste.

2) Simmer uncovered for 30–45 minutes, adding more water as necessary. Remove the onion, add butter, and simmer for an additional 5 minutes. Correct seasonings.

3) Remove heads, legs, and necks from the squab; season squab inside and out with salt and pepper. Truss wings with thread. Wrap each squab with a slice of bacon and fasten with toothpicks.

4) Place squab in an oiled, heated baking pan. Pour clarified butter over squab and place the pan in a preheated oven (400°F/200°C). Roast for 8 minutes, basting occasionally. Remove the pan from the oven and remove bacon from the squab. Cover the squab with foil and return to oven. Roast for a further 5–6 minutes at a very high temperature (480°F/250°C).

5) Place squab on a heated platter and keep warm. Skim excess fat from pan, deglaze the pan with Bordelaise Sauce. Strain, and skim the fat from the surface. Season with salt and pepper to taste.

6) To serve:
Bone and slice the squab. Spoon lentils onto heated serving plates and arrange squab slices on top. Layer pastry slices, spinach and sautéed vegetable to form 4 millefeuilles. Top with a little thyme. Arrange one on each of the plates, spoon on Bordelaise Sauce and serve immediately.

Cailles sous la Cendre

(Roast quail in flaky pastry with Périgueux sauce)
FONTAINEBLEAU

Ingredients (Serves 4)

4 quails (about 1/4 pound/
   100–125 g each)
4 tbsp/60 g fresh foie gras
salt and pepper to taste
1 pound/500 g Puff Pastry
   (see recipe, p. 170)
1 egg yolk, beaten
watercress to garnish
Périgueux Sauce (see recipe,
   p. 169)

Preparation time: 2-1/2 hours
Cooking time: 15 minutes

1) Cut the quail open along the spine and remove all the bones except the leg bones. (This is extremely labor intensive—your butcher may be able to provide boned quail.)

2) Clean the quails and then stuff them with foie gras. Truss closed with a needle and thread. Season with salt and pepper and bake at 480°F/250°C until lightly browned (about 10–15 minutes). Reduce oven to 375°F/190°C after the first 5 minutes. Set aside to cool.

3) When the quails are quite cold, cover them with pastry. Roll out the pastry into a large square, 1/4-inch/6-mm thick. Cut into 4 smaller squares and wrap each quail in a pastry square, tucking the edges under the birds. Glaze pastry with beaten egg yolk, then bake at 400°F/200°C for 15 minutes, or until golden brown.

4) Transfer quail to a serving platter and garnish with watercress. Serve with Périgueux Sauce, sautéed string beans, sautéed champignon and morel mushrooms, and grilled tomatoes.

Jambonette de Volaille Homardine

(Chicken with lobster)

FONTAINEBLEAU

Ingredients (Serves 4)

4 small live lobsters (about 1/2 pound / 250 g each with shell)

10 cups / 2-1/2 liters Court Bouillon (see recipe, p. 167)

4 cups/1 liter Lobster Sauce (see recipe, p. 168)

1 small chicken (about 1-1/2 pounds/750 g)

salt and pepper to taste

3 tbsp/45 g butter

1 garlic clove, crushed

1 tbsp sliced shallots

4 tsp brandy

60 ml dry white wine

1/2 cup / 125 ml Chicken Stock (see recipe, p. 166)

1/4 cup / 60 ml heavy (double) cream

Garnish:

fresh tarragon

about 20 green and white asparagus spears, boiled

Preparation time: about 1-1/2 hours

1) Cook lobsters in boiling Court Bouillon for 12 minutes. Remove, drain and cool until easy to handle. Reserve the Court Bouillon for the stock. Remove pincers and tail meat. Reserve 2 pincers and 3 thick slices of the tail for each plate. Use the heads and shells for Lobster Sauce.

2) Chicken rolls:
Remove the breast and thigh meat from the bones, and cut into 8 neat pieces. Form the meat into 8 rolls with the skin on the outside. Sprinkle with a little salt and pepper. Wrap in plastic wrap, tying the openings firmly with string.

3) Put the chicken rolls in a lidded steamer and steam for 12–13 minutes. Remove, cut string and remove plastic wrap. Melt 1 tbsp/15 g butter in a pan. Sauté chicken gently until the skin is golden brown. Lift out chicken rolls and keep warm.

4) Add the shallots and garlic to the butter in the pan and sauté for a minute or so. Sprinkle with brandy and ignite. After the flame has died down, pour in the white wine and cook until reduced by half. Add the Chicken Stock, reduce slightly then add 1/2 cup/125–150 ml of the Lobster Stock.

5) Heat the mixture and strain. Stir in the cream and season with salt and pepper. Gradually whisk in remaining 2 tbsp butter, beating well after each addition.

6) To serve:
Arrange 2 lobster pincers (be sure to crack them first), 2 chicken rolls and 3 slices of lobster on each serving plate. Top with a sprig of tarragon. Cut the tips from the asparagus spears and thinly slice the stems diagonally. Arrange tips and slices on each plate, spoon on the Lobster Sauce and serve.

Poulet aux morilles à la Crème
(Chicken with morel mushrooms and cream sauce)

FONTAINEBLEAU

Ingredients (Serves 4)

2 ounces / 50–60 g dried or 1/4 pound/125 g fresh morel mushrooms (shiitake may be substituted)

1 cup/250 ml Chicken Stock (see recipe, p. 166), optional

4 tbsp/60 g butter

1 whole chicken (about 2-1/2 pounds/1.2 kilos)

1 tbsp salad oil

2 tbsp finely chopped shallots

1/2 cup/125 ml white port wine or semi-sweet sherry

2 cups/500 ml heavy (double) cream

salt and pepper to taste

Garnish:

Mixed vegetables — carrot, pumpkin, zucchini (courgette), *daikon* (Japanese radish)

1 truffle

chervil

Preparation time: 30 minutes (but dried morels need to be soaked overnight)

Cooking time: 30 minutes

1) Soak dried mushrooms, if using, in lukewarm water until they soften (overnight for morels, about 15 minutes for shiitake). Trim the tough stems and place in a pan with water or Chicken Stock to cover and 1 tbsp butter. Simmer over a low heat until tender, about 10 minutes. Strain and reserve mushrooms and juice.

2) Remove the breast and thigh meat from the chicken and cut into 4 neat portions. Season with salt and pepper. Heat 1 tbsp oil in a large skillet (frying pan) and sauté chicken until golden brown on both sides. Remove chicken and keep warm.

3) Pour off the oil from skillet. Add 1 tbsp butter and sauté chopped shallots until transparent. Add the port wine to the pan and mix with the shallots. Add the sautéed chicken pieces and reserved mushroom cooking juices. Add cream and simmer, uncovered, for about 15 minutes, or until chicken is cooked through.

4) Remove chicken from skillet and keep warm. Strain sauce and whisk in remaining 2 tbsp butter. Season to taste.

5) To serve:
Cut the vegetables and truffle into fine julienne (matchstick) strips. Blanch the julienne vegetables in boiling salted water. Drain and stir in the truffle strips. Place a spoonful of this mixture in the center of each serving plate. Place a chicken piece on top, spoon the sauce around and garnish with the reserved morels and chervil.

Ris de Veau Talleyrand

(Sweetbreads with wine sauce and truffles)
FONTAINEBLEAU

Ingredients (Serves 4)

4 sweetbreads, soaked, cleaned and trimmed (see p. 142 for method)

salt and pepper to taste

5 tbsp/60 g butter

1 tbsp salad oil

2 ounces/50 g each carrots, onion and cucumber, peeled and shaped into small balls

1/2 cup/125 ml Madeira (a dry sherry may be substituted)

1/2 cup/125 ml Veal Stock (see recipe, p. 166)

1 cup/250 ml Périgueux Sauce (see recipe, p. 169)

1/2 pound/250 g fresh foie gras, diced into 1/2-inch/ 1-cm cubes

1/4 pound/125 g macaroni, boiled until tender but still firm

1-1/2 ounces/40 g truffles, finely shredded

1-1/2 ounces/40 g Gruyère, Parmesan, or Emmenthal cheese, finely grated

fresh tarragon to garnish

Preparation time: Several hours
Cooking time: 15 minutes

1) Slice the sweetbreads into neat rounds and season lightly. Heat half the butter and the oil in a skillet (frying pan) and sauté the sweetbreads until golden, 3–4 minutes on each side.

2) Sauté onions and carrots with butter in an ovenproof casserole until soft. Place sweetbreads on top of vegetables and pour Madeira and Veal Stock over all. Braise covered in a preheated oven (250°F/120°C) for 15 minutes.

3) Remove the casserole from the oven. Place sweetbreads on a heated platter and keep warm. Reserve the vegetables. Strain the casserole juices, reduce by half and use in preparing Périgueux Sauce.

4) Lightly sauté the foie gras in the remaining butter. Remove and set aside. Add the cooked macaroni to the butter in the pan and toss well. Add the sautéed foie gras, truffles and grated cheese and mix lightly. Season with salt and pepper to taste.

5) To serve:
Spoon a quarter of the macaroni mixture in the center of each heated serving plate and top with sweetbread slices. Pour Périgueux Sauce around the macaroni and sweetbreads and arrange the reserved vegetables around the edge. Place a sprig of tarragon on top of the sweetbreads and serve immediately.

Millefeuilles aux Fraises
(Strawberry millefeuilles)

Ingredients (Serves 8)

3/4 pound/375 g Puff Pastry (see recipe, p. 170)

2 tbsp granulated sugar

1 egg yolk, beaten

1-1/4 cups / 300 ml Crème Chantilly (see recipe, p. 172)

1-1/2 cups / 375 ml Crème Patissière (see recipe, p. 172)

about 20 fresh strawberries

2 tbsp sieved strawberry jam, heated (see Note)

fine strips of orange peel to decorate

4 tbsp slivered (flaked) almonds, toasted

Preparation time: 45 minutes
Cooking time: 25 minutes

1) Prepare the pastry and, after reserving about 10 percent for the decoration, roll out the rest to form a large rectangle about 9 × 10 inch/22 × 25 cm, 1/8-inch/3-mm thick. Transfer to a baking sheet, prick with a fork and refrigerate for 5–10 minutes. Bake for 20 to 25 minutes in a hot oven (400°F/200°C) until golden. Sprinkle granulated sugar over the pastry and return it to the oven briefly, to brown the sugar. Cool on a rack then cut into 3 neat rectangles, each 3 × 9 inch/9 × 24 cm.

2) Roll out the reserved pastry to 1/4-inch/6-mm thickness and cut into rings using a fluted cutter and a slightly smaller plain cutter. Brush with egg yolk to glaze, and bake in the oven for 15 minutes, or until golden brown.

3) Fold 2/3 of the Crème Chantilly into the Crème Patissière and mix gently.

4) Halve strawberries, setting some whole ones aside for decoration. Place half the strawberries on a pastry layer, then spread with half the pastry cream. Place another pastry layer over the cream and cover with remaining strawberry halves and pastry cream. Top with remaining pastry layer.

5) To decorate:
Place remaining Crème Chantilly in a pastry bag fitted with a star nozzle and pipe rosettes onto the pastry layer. Arrange pastry rings and reserved strawberries on top. Brush strawberries with jam and sprinkle with orange peel strips. Coat both sides of the millefeuilles with toasted almond slices.

Note:
1/2 cup/125 ml puréed strawberries thickened with 1 tsp gelatin and flavored with maraschino liqueur or kirsch can be used instead of the jam.

Mont Blanc aux Marrons

(Mont Blanc)

Ingredients (for a 7-inch/18-cm diameter mold)

1 pound/500 g chestnuts, peeled and inner skins removed (see Note)

about 1/2 cup/120–150 g sugar

1/4 vanilla pod or 1/2 tsp vanilla extract

2 tbsp kirsch

Sugar syrup (made from boiling together 1 cup/250 ml water and 1/2 cup/125 g sugar)

1-1/2 cup/375 ml Crème Chantilly (see recipe, p. 172)

chocolate curls

confectioners' sugar

Preparation time: 2 hours

1) Put peeled chestnuts in a deep pan covered with water and bring to a boil. Change water and again bring to a boil, repeating this process one more time. (This should take about 40 minutes.)

2) After water has boiled for the third time, drain. While chestnuts are still very hot, put them in a clean pan with the sugar and vanilla. Cook over medium heat, mashing the chestnuts with a wooden spoon or spatula; reduce heat when necessary to prevent burning. Knead with a wooden spatula until mixture is smooth. Turn out onto a heatproof surface and let cool.

3) Remove the vanilla pod. When the chestnut mixture is partially cool, add kirsch and mix well.

4) Press the mixture through a sieve twice. If not sufficiently smooth, add a little sugar syrup to give a firm piping consistency.

5) Wipe the inside of a mold with damp absorbent paper and sprinkle insides evenly with confectioners' sugar.

6) Using a 1/8-inch/3-mm diameter nozzle, transfer the chestnut mixture to a pastry bag and squeeze out evenly into the mold. When full, press lightly to firm.

7) Turn the mold onto a serving plate and unmold the mixture. Decorate with Crème Chantilly, chocolate curls and confectioners' sugar.

Note:
To peel chestnuts, cut a cross in the shell on the flat side of each nut then place in a pan of cold water, bring to the boil and boil for one minute. Remove and when cool enough to handle remove peel and rub off the inner skin.

Couronne des Pommes au Caramel

(Caramel and apple ring cake)

Ingredients (Serves 6–8)

unsalted butter for greasing

5 medium tart apples e.g. Granny Smiths

juice and grated peel of one lemon

1 cup/250 g sugar

1/4 cup/60 ml water

6 ounces/175 g Puff Pastry (see recipe, p. 170)

1 egg yolk, beaten

chopped pistachios to decorate

Preparation time: 1 hour
Cooking time: 30 minutes

1) Butter an 8-inch/21-cm ring mold. Cut apples into 6 segments each, removing the core and the peel. Cut each segment into 2 to 3 slices slantwise. Sprinkle with lemon juice to prevent them from browning.

2) Gently heat the sugar and water in a saucepan, stirring constantly until sugar has dissolved. Bring to the boil and boil without stirring until sugar changes color and caramelizes. Take care not to overbrown the caramel. Remove from heat immediately.

3) Coat the bottom of the mold with 2 tbsp caramel. Add the apple slices to the remaining caramel (take care or the caramel will splatter), then heat gently in the saucepan until the apple juices have dissolved the caramel and the caramel has colored the apple pieces. Stir in grated lemon peel and strain, using a large mesh strainer, to separate the apples from the sauce. Reserve the sauce. Cool the apples then arrange them in the mold, pressing down firmly.

4) Roll out the pastry into a square about 1/4-inch/5-mm thick and 8-inch/21-cm wide. Place over the apples and press down firmly, brush with egg yolk to glaze. Let the pastry rest for a few minutes in the refrigerator then trim any overhanging dough from the rims of the mold with a knife. Prick the dough with a sharp knife and let it rest in the refrigerator for a further 10 to 15 minutes.

5) Place on the middle shelf of a preheated hot oven (400°F/200°C). Place the mold on a larger plate to catch any overflow. Bake for 25 to 30 minutes until the pastry is golden brown.

6) Leave in the mold to set for 5–10 minutes then place a serving plate over the ring and tap the bottom of the pan to unmold. Boil reserved caramel sauce until slightly reduced and spread over apples. When the couronne is cold sprinkle with chopped pistachios.

Omelette Norvégienne

(Baked meringue and ice cream cake)

Ingredients (Serves 10)

1 pound/400 g plain Genoise
  cake (see recipe, p.171)
3 pints/1.5 liters ice cream
  (see Note)

Meringue:
10 egg whites
1-2/3 cups/400 g granulated
  sugar
confectioners' sugar, strawberry slices and candied
  violets to decorate
rum to flambé (optional)

Preparation time: 1 hour
Cooking time: 5 minutes

1) Cover the bottom of an oval ovenproof serving platter with 1-inch/2.5-cm thick slices of cake. Mound ice cream over the cake in the shape of a folded omelette. Arrange 1/2-inch/1-cm thick slices of cake on top of the ice cream. Place in a freezer to firm.

2) Beat egg whites until soft peaks form. Gradually add the sugar and beat until mixture becomes stiff. Coat the cake and ice cream with three quarters of the meringue. Place the remainder in a pastry bag fitted with a star nozzle and use to decorate the dessert. Place in a very hot oven (450°F/230°C) until golden, about 5 minutes (check often to avoid burning).

3) Decorate with strawberry slices and candied voilets, and sprinkle with confectioners' sugar. Serve immediately. If you want to flambé the dessert, heat the rum gently, pour it over the meringue, ignite, and serve flaming.

Note:
Two flavors of ice cream can be used; cover the cake slices with one flavor and firm in the freezer before adding the second. The ice cream layers could be separated with a layer of fresh or puréed fruit; freeze the fruit before adding the top layer of ice cream.

Charlotte Royale

(Charlotte Royale)

Ingredients (Serves 8)

1 pound/400 g plain Genoise cake (see recipe, p.171) baked in a 12 × 14-inch/ 30 × 35-cm jelly roll pan (Swiss roll tin) or baking pan

4 tbsp apricot or raspberry jam

a few drops red food coloring

Vanilla Bavarian Cream:

1-1/4 cups/300 ml milk

1/2 vanilla pod

2 tbsp/12 g unflavored gelatin, softened in a little cold water

1/4 cup/60 ml hot water

3 egg yolks

1/3 cup/75 g sugar

1-1/4 cups/300 ml heavy (double) cream

unsalted butter for greasing

a little whipped cream or Crème Chantilly (see recipe, p.172) to decorate

Preparation time: 1 hour (Needs to be made the day before serving)

1) Genoise Roll:
Strain the jam and add enough food coloring to give a vivid color. Spread the strained jam over the Genoise and roll tightly starting from a longer side (the diameter should be about 1-1/4 inches/3 cm). Wrap the roll with waxed paper and refrigerate, outside edge down, for at least an hour, or until it holds its form.

2) Vanilla Bavarian Cream:
Pour milk into a saucepan, add the vanilla pod, broken in two, and bring to boiling point (but do not allow it to boil). Add the softened gelatin to the milk and stir until dissolved. Let it cool slightly.

3) Combine egg yolks and half the sugar in a bowl and beat well with a whisk or electric mixer until pale and thick. Gradually whisk in the cooled milk.

4) Return the mixture to the saucepan. Heat very gently over a low heat for about 3 minutes, stirring constantly, until the mixture is very hot to the touch, but not boiling. It should be thick enough to coat the back of the spoon.

5) Transfer the mixture to a mixing bowl. Place the bowl in a basin of ice water and leave to cool, stirring occasionally.

6) Whip the cream with the remaining sugar until thick but not in stiff peaks. When gelatin mixture has just begun to thicken, carefully fold in the sweetened whipped cream.

7) Cut the rolled Genoise into slices about 1/2-inch/1-cm thick. Grease the sides and base of a 7-inch/18-cm mold or cake tin with unsalted butter. Line the mold with the Genoise slices to make an attractive pattern. Pour in the Bavarian Cream, cover and refrigerate overnight.

8) Unmold the Charlotte onto a serving plate (it may be necessary to stand the mold in hot water for a minute or two). Brush the Charlotte with additional apricot jam if desired and decorate with cream or Crème Chantilly.

Note: A ready-made sponge cake can be substituted for the Genoise but it will result in a much sweeter dessert.

Gâteau d'Anniversaire
(Birthday cake)

Ingredients (Serves 8–12)

Syrup:
1 cup/250 ml water
1/2 cup/125 g sugar
3 tbsp brandy

Chocolate ganache:
1-1/2 cups/375 ml heavy (double) cream
3/4 pound/375 g Couverture (confectioners' chocolate) or bitter (dark) chocolate, broken into small pieces
8-inch/20-cm chocolate Genoise cake, (see recipe, p. 171)
chocolate flowers and leaves, fresh flowers and leaves or marzipan flowers and leaves to decorate

Preparation time: 45 minutes

1) Syrup:
Place the water and sugar in a saucepan and heat gently, stirring, until sugar has dissolved. Bring to the boil, without stirring, and boil until syrupy. Remove from the heat and stir in the brandy. Cool before using.

2) Chocolate ganache:
Heat the cream in a saucepan until just below boiling point. Add the chocolate, reduce the heat to low and whisk constantly until the chocolate has dissolved. Do not boil the mixture. Remove from the heat, transfer to a bowl and cool, then refrigerate until required. (You can speed up the cooling process by spreading the ganache over a marble slab or stainless steel surface.) Ganache must be cooled before using.

3) Cut the cold cake into 3 even layers and generously brush each layer with syrup. Place the bowl of ganache over a pan of hot water and heat gently until soft.

4) Spread a quarter of the ganache over a layer of cake; top with a second layer. Spread this with another quarter of ganache and top with the remaining ganache. Transfer to a serving plate and decorate with flowers and leaves, and any desired piping.

Basic Recipes

Veal Stock

Ingredients (Makes about 12 cups/3 liters)

5 pounds/2.5 kg veal bones
1/2 pound/250 g carrots, scrubbed and coarsely sliced
2 large onions, peeled and coarsely sliced
5 quarts/5 liters cold water
1 bouquet garni
salt and pepper to taste

Preparation time: 5 minutes
Cooking time: 1-1/2 hours

1) Sauté bones in a greased pan. When they are slightly brown, add vegetables. Continue to sauté for 20 minutes over medium heat, then drain off fat through a sieve.

2) Place drained bones and vegetables in a deep stock pot, add water and bring to the boil. Skim the surface and continue to simmer over low heat for about an hour until reduced by half. Strain through a sieve, then drag a paper towel over the surface to remove any excess fat. Season with salt and pepper.

Notes:
To make clear stock, be sure to start with cold water and simmer the stock very slowly over a very low heat.
Stock will keep in the refrigerator for about one week. It is a good idea to make large quantities of stock and freeze any you don't need immediately.

Fish Stock

Ingredients (Makes about 6 cups/1.5 liters)

1 pound/500 g fish bones and heads from white-fleshed fish, washed
1 carrot, peeled and sliced
1 medium onion, sliced
8 cups/2 liters water
1 bay leaf
salt and pepper to taste

Preparation time: 5 minutes
Cooking time: 20 minutes

1) Place fish bones, heads, and water in a deep saucepan and bring to a boil over high heat. Skim the surface and add remaining ingredients. Reduce heat and simmer for 15 minutes.

2) Strain through a cotton cloth. Drag a sheet of paper towel over the surface to remove excess fat. Season with salt and pepper.

Note:
To make clear stock, wash bones and heads well and be sure not to simmer too long over low heat.

Beef or Chicken Stock

Ingredients (Makes about 5 cups/1-1/4 liters)

2 pounds/1 kg beef shank or 1 chicken carcass
1 carrot, peeled and coarsely chopped
1 medium onion, coarsely chopped
1 stalk celery, coarsely chopped
10 cups/2.5 liters water
1–2 bay leaves
2 tsp finely chopped parsley
salt and pepper to taste

Preparation time: 5 minutes
Cooking time: 1-1/2 hours

1) Place beef or chicken and water in a deep saucepan and bring to a boil over high heat. Skim the surface.

2) Add all remaining ingredients to the pan

and return to the boil. Skim the surface and reduce heat. Simmer over low heat for about 1-1/2 hours.

3) Strain slowly through a cotton cloth. Drag a paper towel over the surface to remove excess fat.

Note:
To clarify stock, allow to cool then remove fat from the surface. Place stock in a pan with 2 lightly beaten egg whites and 2 crushed egg shells. Bring slowly to the boil, whisking occasionally. Reduce heat and simmer for 20 minutes. Strain through a cotton cloth and use.

Court Bouillon

A light, quickly made, acidulated vegetable stock used for poaching fish, shellfish, and sometimes meat and vegetables.

Ingredients (Makes 10 cups/2.5 liters)

10 cups/2.5 liters water
1/2 pound/250 g carrots
1/2 pound/250 g onions
1 cup/250 ml vinegar (see Notes)
1-1/2 tbsp/25 g salt (see Notes)
1 bay leaf
1 bunch parsley
a pinch of thyme
salt and pepper to taste

Preparation time: 5 minutes
Cooking time: 15 minutes

1) Wash and chop vegetables coarsely. Place in a saucepan filled with the water and remaining ingredients. Bring to a boil over high heat. As the stock cooks, skim the surface until clear, then reduce the heat and simmer for 15 minutes. Strain and season bouillon to taste.

Notes:
The quantities for bouillon can easily be increased or reduced. A dry white wine can be substituted for all but 2 tbsp of the vinegar.
Reduce the amount of salt used if the fish is to be cooled in the bouillon and eaten cold.

Béchamel Sauce

Ingredients (Makes 1 cup/250 ml)

2 tbsp/30 g butter
2 tbsp flour, sifted
1 cup/250 ml hot milk
1/2 bay leaf
salt and pepper to taste

Preparation time: 10 minutes
Cooking time: 30 minutes

1) Melt butter in an ovenproof saucepan over low heat. Add flour and stir with a wooden spoon to form a roux. Stir over low heat for a minute or so until combined and pasty. Remove from heat.

2) Pour in a quarter of the heated milk at a time, stirring with a wire whisk until smooth. Repeat process until all liquid is blended. Add bay leaf. Return to low heat and stir constantly until sauce thickens. Remove bay leaf and serve.

Notes:
In order to avoid lumps, be sure not to add the heated milk too gradually. Pour in a quarter at a time and stir with a wire whisk until smooth.
If you need the sauce quickly, gradually whisk in the milk and bay leaf then return the pan to a moderate heat. Bring to the boil, stirring constantly. Reduce heat and continue to boil for 1–2 minutes. Season to taste.

Demi-glace Sauce

The classic brown or glace sauce is made by simmering browned meat bones and stock for many hours until it reaches a syrupy consistency. This sauce is only cooked for about half the time, so it is called Demi-(half) glace Sauce.

Ingredients (Makes about 8 cups/2 liters)

3/4 pound/375 g tough and sinewy cuts of beef, cut in small pieces
Bones from 1 chicken carcass, disjointed or crushed
1/2 carrot, coarsely chopped
1/2 onion, coarsely chopped

1 clove of garlic, crushed
5–6 tbsp flour, sifted
12 cups/3 liters Beef Stock (see recipe, p. 166)
1/2 cup/125 ml tomato purée
1 bay leaf
salt and pepper to taste

Preparation time: 20 minutes
Cooking time: 2 hours

1) Sauté meat, chicken bones, carrot, onion and garlic in a large greased pan or skillet over high heat.

2) When ingredients begin to color, add sifted flour and continue to sauté until contents turn brown. Stir in some Beef Stock to dissolve pan drippings, scraping burned spots with a wooden spoon.

3) Transfer to a large saucepan. Add remaining Beef Stock, tomato purée and bay leaf, and bring to a boil over high heat. Skim the surface and reduce heat. Simmer very gently, stirring occasionally for 2 hours.

4) Strain and season to taste.

Notes:
A spoonful of caramel or soy sauce produces an even richer color.
Any Demi-glace Sauce not needed immediately can be frozen.

Rémoulade Sauce

Ingredients (Makes 1 cup/250 ml)

1 cup/250 ml good quality mayonnaise
2 tbsp chopped onion
1-1/2 tbsp chopped cucumber pickles
1 tbsp chopped capers
1/2 tsp chopped parsley
1 tbsp lemon juice
anchovy paste to taste

Preparation time: 5 minutes

Mix mayonnaise with the other ingredients just before serving.

Lobster Sauce

Ingredients (Makes 4 cups/1 liter)

heads and shells of 4 small lobsters
1 onion, chopped
1 carrot, diced
1 cup/100 g white mushrooms, chopped
1/4 cup/60 ml Cognac
1/2 cup/125 ml dry white wine
1 tbsp tomato purée
8 cups/2 liters Court Bouillon (see recipe, p. 167)
1 sprig thyme
1 bay leaf
6 black peppercorns

Cooking time: 1-1/4 hours

1) Sauté the onion, carrot, and mushrooms with the reserved lobster heads and shells. Flambé with cognac then deglaze the pan with the white wine.

2) Stir in the tomato purée, add 8 cups/2 liters reserved Court Bouillon or water, bring to the boil and simmer, uncovered, with thyme, a bay leaf, and black pepper, for one hour. Strain.

Hollandaise Sauce

Ingredients (Makes about 1-1/2 cups/250–375 ml)

2 tbsp white vinegar
2 tbsp water
1-1/3 cup/250 g butter
3 egg yolks

Preparation time: 20 minutes

1) Boil vinegar and water in a small pan until reduced by half, then cool. Melt butter in a double boiler.

2) Beat egg yolks well and add cooled liquid. Place in a bowl over boiling water or in a double boiler and beat constantly with a whisk or hand mixer until the mixture has the consistency of heavy cream.

3) Skim the sediment from the surface of the melted butter. Add butter to the egg yolk mixture one spoon at a time, whisking thoroughly after each addition. (Be careful not to mix in the impurities from the bottom of the melted butter.)

Périgueux Sauce

Ingredients (Makes about 1-1/2 cups/375 ml)

3/4 cup/200 ml Demi-glace Sauce (see recipe, p. 167)
6 tbsp/100 ml Veal Stock (see recipe, p. 166)
2 tbsp juice from truffle bottle or can
6 tbsp/100 ml Madeira (a dry sherry may be substituted)
1-1/2 ounces/40 g truffles, finely diced
1 tbsp softened butter
salt and pepper to taste

Preparation time: 10 minutes
Cooking time: 10 minutes + Demi-glace Sauce and Veal Stock

1) Mix Demi-glace Sauce, Veal Stock, and truffle juice in a pan, and bring to a boil. Add Madeira and simmer for 5 minutes, stirring with a wooden spoon.

2) Add diced truffles then gradually whisk in the butter to increase the volume of sauce. Add any pan juices available and season with salt and pepper to taste.

Jus d'Agneau

Ingredients (Makes about 2 cups/500 ml)

1 pound/500 g lamb bones and gristle (use the trimmings from lamb cutlets)
salad oil for frying
1 large onion, peeled and coarsely chopped
1 stalk celery, coarsely chopped
2 tbsp shallot, finely sliced
1 tsp crushed garlic
3 tbsp white wine
4 cups/1 liter Beef Stock (see recipe, p. 166)
1 tomato, peeled, seeded, and diced

1 bouquet garni
1 tsp fresh or a pinch of dried tarragon
1 or 2 fresh or a pinch of dried basil leaves
salt and pepper to taste

Preparation time: 10 minutes
Cooking time: 3-1/2 hours

1) Sauté bones and gristle in a greased frying pan until all the moisture is gone and fat begins to run. Add a little oil, onion and celery and continue to sauté until mixture browns thoroughly. Strain fat through a sieve, reserve bones and vegetables.

2) Using the strained oil, sauté sliced shallot briefly in a large saucepan without allowing it to color, then add garlic and cook for an additional 2–3 minutes. Add reserved browned bones and vegetables, along with the white wine and stock. Bring to a boil. Add the diced tomato, herbs and seasonings.

3) Simmer for 3 hours, occasionally skimming the surface. Strain through a clean linen towel or fine sieve and correct seasoning with salt and pepper.

Madeira Sauce

Ingredients (Makes about 2 cups/500 ml)

salad oil for frying
1/2 pound/250 g shallots, finely chopped
1/4 bottle Madeira (a dry sherry can be substituted)
2 quarts/2 liters Veal Stock (see recipe, p. 166)
salt and pepper to taste

Preparation time: 5 minutes
Cooking time: 1 hour

1) Heat oil in a pan, sauté the shallots briefly without allowing them to color. Add Madeira and simmer until the volume is reduced by two thirds. Pour in Veal Stock.

2) Bring to a boil, skim the surface. Reduce heat and simmer until original volume is reduced by three quarters. Strain and season to taste.

Sauce Suprême aux Truffes

Ingredients (Makes about 3 cups/750 ml)

4 tbsp/50 g butter
4 tbsp flour
2-1/2 cups/600 ml hot Veal Stock (see recipe, p. 166)
generous 3/4 cup/200 ml heavy cream
1-1/2 ounces/40 g truffles, finely diced
salt and pepper to taste
juice from truffle bottle or can to taste

Preparation time: 5 minutes
Cooking time: 20 minutes + Veal Stock

1) Melt butter over low heat and add flour to make a roux. Stir constantly for about 3 minutes without allowing to color. Whisk in Veal Stock and any pan juices available. Cook over low heat for 20 minutes, stirring constantly. Do not allow to boil.

2) Add cream and truffle juice to taste and heat through. Strain sauce through a sieve. Add diced truffles and season with salt and pepper.

Bordelaise Sauce

Ingredients (Makes about 1 cup/250 ml)

2 tbsp chopped shallots
1/4 tsp coarsely ground black pepper
1/2 tsp dried thyme
1/2 tsp bay leaf
6 tbsp/100 ml red wine
6 tbsp/100 ml Demi-glace Sauce (see recipe, p. 167)
6 tbsp/100 ml Veal Stock (see recipe, p. 166)
salt to taste

Preparation time: 5 minutes
Cooking time: 10 minutes + Demi-glace Sauce and Veal Stock

1) Sauté chopped shallot in a hot greased pan for 3 minutes. Add coarsely ground pepper, thyme, bay leaf and red wine. Simmer until volume is reduced by half.

2) Add Demi-glace Sauce and stock to the shallot-wine reduction. Simmer for 5 minutes, stirring with a wooden spoon. Strain and serve.

Saffron Rice

Ingredients (Makes 2 cups rice)

2 tbsp/30 g butter
1 onion, finely chopped
1 cup long-grain rice, washed
pinch saffron strands, soaked in 1 tbsp hot water
2 cups/500 ml boiling water or Fish Stock

Cooking time: 45 minutes

1) Melt butter in a deep skillet (frying pan) or saucepan and sauté chopped onions until transparent. Add rice to pan and stir until well mixed. Add the saffron and soaking liquid, and the water or stock.

2) Cover, bring to the boil, reduce heat slightly and cook for about 20 minutes. Check to see if all liquid has been absorbed (shallow depressions, called eyes, should appear on the top of the rice when done). When all the liquid has been absorbed remove from heat and allow to stand covered for 5 minutes or until serving.

Note:
A teaspoon of turmeric may be used in place of saffron.

Imperial Puff Pastry

Ingredients (Makes about 2 pounds/1 kg)

4 cups/530 g flour
1 tsp salt or to taste
2 cups/375 g butter
about 2 cups/500 ml iced water

Preparation time: at least 1 hour

1) Using your finger tips or a pastry blender, combine 3-3/4 cups/500 g flour, salt and 1-1/3 cup/250 g butter until mixture resembles

breadcrumbs. Sprinkle one cup of water over the mixture and toss with 2 forks or a pastry blender, adding more water as necessary until dough can be formed into a ball with your hands. Place it, covered, in the refrigerator, for at least 15 minutes.

2) Meanwhile, beat the remaining 2/3 cup/ 125 g butter with 1/4 cup/30 g of flour until mixture forms a pasty consistency. Shape into a square about 1/4-inch/6-mm thick, wrap in wax paper, and place in refrigerator to cool.

3) Remove dough from refrigerator and quickly roll out, on a lightly floured surface, into an oblong shape about 1/8-inch/3-mm thick. Place the butter-flour square in the center of the dough. Fold the long sides of the dough over the butter-flour square. Seal the slightly overlapping edges by pressing lightly with the rolling pin. Turn the pastry so the folds are at the side and roll out again, from top to bottom, to an oblong about 1/4-inch/6-mm thick. Fold as before and repeat. Wrap in wax paper and place in refrigerator for 15 minutes.

4) Remove and roll out twice more, folding and turning the pastry round each time. Refrigerate for a further 15 minutes and roll out the pastry twice more. Wrap in wax paper and let the pastry rest in refrigerator for at least 15 minutes before using. The longer the pastry is allowed to rest in the refrigerator the more delicate the pastry will be.

Notes:
If using this recipe for sweet dishes, reduce the amount of salt used.
Commercially prepared puff pastry may be substituted.

Pommes de Terre à la Lyonnaise

Ingredients (Serves 4–6)

2 small onions, thinly sliced
butter for frying
6 medium potatoes, peeled
salt and pepper to taste
finely chopped parsley to garnish

Preparation time: 10 minutes

Cooking time: 30 minutes

1) Sauté sliced onions in butter until they begin to color. Reserve.

2) Parboil potatoes and drain. When cool enough to handle, peel and quarter, then cut into thin slices. Sauté potatoes in butter to add color and flavor.

3) Add onions to the pan and toss lightly to mix. Season with salt and pepper and sprinkle with chopped parsley. Serve immediately.

Genoise

Genoise, or Genoese cake, is a European sponge cake made with butter but it contains much less sugar than American sponge cake.

Ingredients (Makes scant 1 pound/400 g)

4 eggs
1/2 cup/125 g sugar
1 cup/125 g flour, sifted
1-1/2 tbsp/25 g butter, melted (see Note)
Butter for greasing the pan.

Preparation time: 20 minutes
Cooking time: 25 minutes

1) Grease an 8-inch/20-cm round tin or a 12 × 14-inch/30 × 35-cm shallow baking pan with softened butter using your fingers or a brush, and line with non-stick baking parchment.

2) Break eggs into a bowl and stand it over a pan of hot water. Beat with a whisk or electric beater, then gradually add the sugar. Continue to beat until the mixture is light in color and thick enough to leave a trail when the whisk is lifted.

3) Fold the sifted flour into the mixture with a metal spoon or spatula. When well blended, add the melted butter and gently fold into the batter.

4) Pour the batter into the prepared pan and tap the bottom of the pan on the counter lightly to eliminate any excess air. Bake in a

preheated oven (350°F/180°C) for 25 minutes. The Genoise is cooked if it springs back when pressed with your finger tips or if a fine skewer inserted in the center comes out clean.

5) Cool the Genoise for a few minutes on a rack. Loosen carefully from the pan and place the Genoise upside-down on a wooden board. Use when cold.

Note:
Clarified butter gives best results; to clarify butter heat butter in a pan until melted and frothy; do not brown. Transfer to a bowl and cool. When solid, scrape away the sediment from the base of the butter and discard. For chocolate Genoise, use 4/5 cup/100 g flour sifted with 1/5 cup/20–25 g of cocoa.

Crème Patissière
(Pastry or Custard Cream)

Ingredients (Makes about 1-1/2 cups/375 ml)

2 egg yolks
1 cup/250 ml milk
1/4 cup/60 g sugar
1/4 vanilla pod
3 tbsp/30 g cornstarch, sifted
1 tbsp/15 g butter

Preparation time: 5 minutes
Cooking time: 10 minutes

1) In a bowl, beat together the egg yolks with half the sugar and the cornstarch.

2) Pour the milk into a heavy saucepan and add the remaining sugar and vanilla pod. Bring to boiling point, but do not allow to boil. Quickly add to the egg yolk mixture, whisking thoroughly. Strain.

3) Return the mixture to the saucepan, or use a double boiler, and heat gently, stirring constantly with a wooden spoon. Do not allow the mixture to boil. After the mixture thickens, continue mixing until custard is soft and smooth. Remove from heat and beat in the butter.

4) Cover the surface with waxed paper and allow custard to cool in the saucepan. (You can spread the custard over a marble slab if you want it to cool quickly).

Crème Chantilly
(Sweetened whipped cream)

Ingredients (Makes 4 cups/1 liter)

4 cups/1 liter whipping cream
1/3 cup/80 g sugar
1 tbsp liqueur or vanilla extract

Preparation time: 5 minutes

1) Pour cream into a bowl, add the sugar and flavoring, and whip with a balloon whisk while holding the bowl of cream in a basin of ice.

2) The cream is true Crème Chantilly when it is stiff enough to form peaks and hold its shape when squeezed from a pastry bag.

Note:
Additional liqueur can be added to taste.

INDEX

TEXT INDEX

Allied Ocupation, 35, 36
alternate attendance, 13–14
American embassy, 34
Ando Hiroshige. *See* Hiroshige
architecture, Japanese, 7
artworks, 9

bakery, 43, 67
ballrooms, 20–21
bento, 85
La Brasserie, 75–76
breakfast service, 67–68
buffets, 68, 76–77

Chaliapin, Fyodor, 70–71
Chinese cuisine, 84
Cycles Coffee Shop, 43

"Dawn" mural, 9
Diet, 22
dinner dances, 32
doormen, 52

Earthquake resistance, 24–25, 28–30
Edo. *See* Tokyo
Emperor Hirohito, funeral of, 45–46
Ende, Bockman and Company, 19, 20
Endo, Arata, 26, 28
Escoffier, Auguste, 74

fires, 24, 26
Flaig, Emil, 22
Fontainebleau, 64, 79–80
Fujii, Hiroshi, 42
furnishings and equipment, 20, 28, 42, 45, 51

Gargantua, 43
Ginza, 13, 15
Great Kanto Earthquake, 28–31
guests, 8–9, 21, 42

Hayashi, Aisaku, 24, 26
Hiroshige, 13
Horakuzen, 82
hotels: early Japanese, 14, 15–16; Hotel Metropole, 22; Hotel Okura, 35

Imperial Hotel, design and construction of the first, 19–20; design and construction of the second, 24–28; design and construction of the third, 40; location of, 8, 10, 19, management of, 19, 40, 42
Imperial Household Ministry (Agency), 19, 22, 46, 51–52
Imperial Suite, 51
Imperial Tower, 19, 43–44

inns, 13, 14. *See also* ryokan
Inoue, Kaoru, 18
Inoue, Setsuko, 53
Inumaru, Ichiro, 40–42, 45
Inumaru, Tetsuzo, 28, 31–32, 34–35, 36, 37, 40, 42–43, 56, 72
Isecho, 82
Iseya Chobei, 82
Ishiwatari, Bunjiro, 69
Ito, Takio, 88
Iwasaki Yataro, 19

Japan Tourist Bureau, 22

kaiseki ryori, 82
kitchens, 31, 64, 68
Kitcho, 82–83
Kobe beef, 67, 85–86

laundry, 54
Lobby, 8–10, 28
lounges, 28

MacArthur, Douglas A. 34
Matsubara, Chef, 67
meat supply, 67
Meiji Mura Museum, 38
Meiji Restoration, 13, 15–17, 18
Midway Gardens, 26
Minoshima, Kiyohito, 42, 49
Mori, Chef, 64
Morris, Timothy, 35–36
Murakami, Nobuo, 68–72, 76
Murano, Togo, 80–81

Nadaman, 85–86
Nakata, 84–85
nouvelle cuisine, 75

occupancy rates, 21, 22, 44
Okura, Kihachiro, 18–19, 26, 27
Okura, Kishichiro, 35
Old Imperial Bar, 86–88
Olympic Games (1964), 37, 40, 71–72
Osaka Exposition, 40
Ota, Dokan, 13
oya stonework, 25, 28, 37, 38

Peacock Room, 44–45
Peking Restaurant, 84
Perry, Matthew C., 15
personnel management, 48
Prunier, 78–79

Rainbow Room, 68, 76–77
reception, 53

renovations, 44–45
reservations, 53
restaurants, of the Imperial Hotel, 74–75; La Brasserie, 75–76; Fontainebleau, 79–80; Isecho, 82; Kitcho, 82–83; Nadaman, 85–86; Nakata, 84–85; Peking 84; Prunier, 78–79; Rainbow Room, 76–77; Les Saisons, 77–78; Sushigen, 86; Ten-ichi, 83; Toko-an, 80–81
Ritz, César, 10, 32, 74
Rokumeikan, 16, 19
rugby team, 52
ryokan, 16, 17–18. *See also* inns

Sagoyan, Ivan, 67
Les Saisons, 68, 77–78
Salon de Thé, 45
Savoy Hotel, 10, 15
Seiyoken Hotel, 16
service charges, 48
Shibusawa, Eiichi, 19
Shigemitsu, Mamoru, 34
Shinto ceremonies, 60–61
shokado 82, 85
shopping facilities, 42–43, 44
smorgasbord, 76
staff: conditions of employment for, 45, 48, 52; grading of, 49; number of, 52; training of, 42, 49
stocks, 64
Sugashima, Katsumi, 67
sukiyaki, 86
supply center, 65–67
sushi, 84–85, 86
Sushigen, 86
swimming pools, 28, 43
switchboard, 53–54

Takahashi, Teitaro, 37, 40
Takeya, Toshiko, 34, 49–52
teahouse, 80–81
tempura, 83
Ten-ichi, 83
tipping, 48, 54
Toko-an, 80–81
Tokugawa Iemitsu, 14
Tokugawa Ieyasu, 13
Tokyo, 7, 13–14
Tokyo Hotel, 16
Tomita, Nobuo, 52
tourism, 36–37
travel, in early Japan, 12–13
Tsukiji Hotel, 16
Tsutsui, Chef, 70

Waldorf-Astoria Hotel, 10, 15, 32, 41
Waldorf, William, 15
Watanabe, Yuzuru, 20
weddings, 56–62
World War II, 33–34
Wright, Frank Lloyd, 24–28, 31

Yamaguchi, H. K. S., 26
Yokohama, 15, 16
Yokoyama, M., 21

Zeppelin, catering for the, 33

RECIPE INDEX

Aiguillettes de Canard au Poivre Vert et aux Galettes de Maïs (sliced duck with peppercorn sauce), 128
Andersen Fizz cocktail, 88
apples
  Couronne des Pommes au Caramel (crown of caramel apples), 158
artichokes
  Filets de Sole Murat (sole fillets meunière), 130
avocados
  Crème d'Avocat Glacée à la Bombay (iced avocado soup Bombay-style), 104

beans
  Foie Gras Frais Sauté sur Lit de Haricots Verts (sautéed fresh foie gras and young green beans), 96
  Pigeonneaux Rôtis aux Lentilles Sauce Bordelaise (roast squab with lentils and Bordelaise sauce), 144
  Salade Tiède de Langouste et Ris de Veau Vinaigrette au Curry (warm langouste salad with sweetbreads and curry-flavored dressing), 90
Béchamel Sauce, 167; 102, 114
beef
  Beef stock, 166
  Bifteck à la Chaliapin (Beefsteak Chaliapin), 126
  Cœur de Filet de Bœuf Metternich (fillet of beef Metternich), 116
  Choucroute Garnie à l'Alsacienne (Alsace-style sauerkraut casserole), 120
  Steak Tartare ("La Brasserie" tartar steak), 122
Beurre Noisette, 130
Beurre d'Oursins (sea urchin butter sauce), 94
Bifteck à la Chaliapin (Beefsteak Chaliapin), 126
Bisque de Homard (French lobster bisque), 108
Blanc de Turbot aux Pignes Mesclun de Céleri (grilled turbot with pine nuts and celery), 136
Blanchailles Frites (deep-fried whitebait), 100
Bloody Caesar, 88
Bordelaise Sauce, 170; 144

Cailles sous la Cendre (roast quail in flaky pastry with Périgueux sauce), 146
Caneton Rôti a l'Ananas (roast duck with pineapple), 140
Charlotte Royale, 162
Chateaux turnips, 124
chestnuts
  Mont Blanc aux Marrons (Mont Blanc), 156
chicken. *See* poultry and game
Chocolate ganache, 164
Choucroute Garnie à l'Alsacienne (Alsace-style sauerkraut casserole), 120
cocktails: Andersen Fizz, 88; Bloody Caesar, 88; Mt. Fuji, 88
Cœur de Filet de Bœuf Metternich (fillet of beef Metternich), 116
Coquilles Saint-Jacques Espadon (curried scallops), 98
Côtelettes d'Agneau Poêlées au Confit d'Oignons et Champignons (grilled lamb chops with onions and mushrooms), 138
Couronne des Pommes au Caramel (crown of caramel apples), 158
Court Bouillon, 167
Crème d'Avocat Glacée à la Bombay (iced avocado soup Bombay-style), 104
Crème Chantilly (sweetened whipped cream), 172

Crème Patissière, 172
Curry Dressing, 90
Custard Cream, 172

Demi-glace Sauce, 167
dressings
    Curry, 90
    Rémoulade Sauce, 168
duck. *See* poultry and game

eggs
    Œuf Poché Alexandre 1er (poached egg on brioche
        with caviar and smoked salmon), 102
    Omelette Lorraine (omelette Lorraine-style, with
        cheese and bacon), 118
    Omelette Norvégienne (baked meringue and ice cream
        cake), 160
    Soufflé d'Oursins (soufflé of sea urchin), 94
Escalope de Veau et Ris de Veau à la Crème aux Truffes
    (veal scallops and ris de veau with cream truffle sauce),
    142

Filets de Sole Murat (sole fillets meunière), 130
fish (*See also* seafood)
    Fish Stock, 166
    smoked salmon: Millefeuilles de Saumon Fumé au
        Caviar (millefeuilles of smoked salmon with caviar),
        92; Œuf Poché Alexandre 1er (poached egg on
        brioche with caviar and smoked salmon), 102
    sole: Filets de Sole Murat (sole fillets meunière), 130;
        Suprême de Sole Bonne Femme (fillet of sole Bonne
        Femme), 132
    turbot: Blanc de Turbot aux Pignes Mesclun de Céleri
        (grilled turbot with pine nuts and celery), 136
    whitebait: Blanchailles Frites (deep-fried whitebait),
        100
foie gras
    Cailles sous la Cendre (roast quail in flaky pastry with
        Périgueux sauce), 146
    Foie Gras Frais Sauté sur Lit de Haricots Verts (sautéed
        fresh foie gras and young green beans), 96
    Ris de Veau Talleyrand (sweetbreads with wine sauce
        and truffles), 152

Galettes de Maïs, 128
Gâteau d'Anniversaire (birthday cake), 164
Genoise Cake, 171
    Charlotte Royale, 162
    Gâteau d'Anniversaire (birthday cake), 164
    Omelette Norvégienne (baked meringue and ice cream
        cake), 160
Gratin de Langouste à la Crème (spiny lobster gratin),
    114

Hollandaise Sauce, 168; 102, 114, 132

Imperial Puff Pastry, 170

Jambonette de Volaille Homardine (chicken with lobster),
    148
Jus d'Agneau, 169

lamb
    Côtelettes d'Agneau Poêlées au Confit d'Oignons et
        Champignons (grilled lamb chops with onions and
        mushrooms), 138
    Jus d'Agneau, 169

Noisettes d'Agneau Corolle de Courgettes et Tomates
    (medallions of lamb on a crown of tomatoes and
    zucchinis), 124
lobster. *See* seafood
Lobster Sauce, 168; 148

Madeira Sauce, 169; 116
marrons
    Mont Blanc aux Marrons (Mont Blanc), 156
Millefeuilles aux Fraises (strawberry millefeuilles), 154
Millefeuilles de Saumon Fumé au Caviar (millefeuilles of
    smoked salmon with caviar), 92
Mont Blanc aux Marrons (Mont Blanc), 156
Mt. Fuji cocktail, 88
mushrooms
    Cœur de Filet de Bœuf Metternich (fillet of beef Met-
        ternich), 116
    Coquilles Saint-Jacques Espadon (curried scallops), 98
    Côtelettes d'Agneau Poêlées au Confit d'Oignons et
        Champignons (grilled lamb chops with onions and
        mushrooms), 138
    Gratin de Langouste à la Crème (spiny lobster gratin),
        114
    Poulet aux Morilles à la Crème (chicken with morel
        mushrooms and cream sauce), 150
    Suprême de Sole Bonne Femme (fillets of sole Bonne
        Femme), 32

Noisettes d'Agneau Corolle de Courgettes et Tomates
    (medallions of lamb on a crown of tomatoes and
    zucchinis), 124
Œuf Poché Alexandre 1er (poached egg on brioche with
    caviar and smoked salmon), 102
Omelette Lorraine (omelette Lorraine-style, with cheese
    and bacon), 118
Omelette Norvégienne (baked meringue and ice cream
    cake), 160
onions
    Bifteck à la Chaliapin (Beefsteak Chaliapin), 126
    Côtelettes d'Agneau Poêlées au Confit d'Oignons et
        Champignons (grilled lamb chops with onions and
        mushrooms), 138
    Pommes de Terre à la Lyonnaise, 171
    Soupe à l'Oignon au Gratinée, (French onion soup),
        106
oysters. *See* seafood

Pastry Cream, 172
peaches
    Potage aux Pêches Glacées (iced peach soup), 110
Périgueux Sauce, 169; 96, 146, 152
Pigeonneaux Rôtis aux Lentilles Sauce Bordelaise (roast
    squab with lentils and Bordelaise sauce), 144
Pineapple sauce, 140
Pommes de Terre à la Lyonnaise, 171
Potage aux Huîtres à la Crème (cream of oyster soup),
    112
Potage aux Pêches Glacées (iced peach soup), 110
Potatoes Lyonnaise (Pommes de Terre à la Lyonnaise), 171
Poulet aux Morilles à la Crème (chicken with morel
    mushrooms and cream sauce), 150
poultry and game
    chicken: Chicken Stock, 166; Jambonette de Volaille
        Homardine (chicken with lobster), 148; Poulet
        aux Morilles à la Crème (chicken with morel